BRIEF HISTORY OF
GERMAN
IMMIGRATION INTO
AMERICA

*– from where, to where, why they came
and what they contributed.*

WOLFGANG H VOGEL

BRIEF HISTORY OF GERMAN IMMIGRATION INTO AMERICA – FROM WHERE, TO WHERE, WHY THEY CAME AND WHAT THEY CONTRIBUTED.

iUniverse books may be ordered through booksellers or by contacting:

iUniverse
1663 Liberty Drive
Bloomington, IN 47403
www.iuniverse.com
844-349-9409

Because of the dynamic nature of the Internet, any web addresses or links contained in this book may have changed since publication and may no longer be valid. The views expressed in this work are solely those of the author and do not necessarily reflect the views of the publisher, and the publisher hereby disclaims any responsibility for them.

Any people depicted in stock imagery provided by Getty Images are models, and such images are being used for illustrative purposes only.
Certain stock imagery © Getty Images.

ISBN: 978-1-6632-0741-8 (sc)
ISBN: 978-1-6632-0742-5 (e)

Library of Congress Control Number: 2020918771

Print information available on the last page.

iUniverse rev. date: 10/19/2020

ACKNOWLEDGEMENTS

The Author wishes to thank Ursula Vogel, Britta Vogel, Renate Veeder and Dr. R. Clearfield for their many helpful suggestions.

INTRODUCTION

The United States of America or in short America originated from the immigration of people of all different ethnic backgrounds. It is often called a "Melting Pot". This encompasses immigration of people into this country and their assimilation into one American culture. The words melting plot are derived from a play with the same name which debuted in 1908.While each of these different ethnic groups has a distinct and interesting history, this book focuses on Germany and their residents immigrating, over time, to this country.

In 2014, it was estimated that about 45 million individuals with German ancestry or about 16% of the population lived in this country. More than half of all our counties contain a plurality of residents who describe themselves as German-Americans. This number is most likely larger since many have forgotten or are unaware of their German roots. Of all the immigrants, Germans are on top of the list with 45 million followed by the Irish (36 million)\, Mexicans (32 million), English (27 million) and Italians (17 millions).

The author is also an immigrant from Germany and so is his wife. We both have become American citizens in the meantime. Our alliance and loyalty rests with this country which has been very good to us indeed. Nevertheless, we still remember our roots in Germany and some aspects of this book reflect our German heritage. Since English is the author's second language, the reader might detect a German undertone while reading this book.

Over the years, many of our American friends, colleagues and acquaintances who are of German descent have asked me questions about their ancestors and wondered why they did leave their home country to start a new life in America, what happened to them after their arrivals and what were their contributions to America. Some knew some details like cities where their ancestors came from while other had no knowledge whatsoever except that they somehow originated in Germany, However, they all expressed a desire to learn a bit more about Germany, some of its history and why their ancestors left their home country.

This booklet is a brief history of German immigration into America to provide some general answers to questions like – why did Germans leave Germany or what happened in Germany to make them leave their home country, how easy or tough was their start in their newly chosen country and what did they contribute to the enormous progress this country has made over the years. Since immigrations occurred not smoothly but often in big waves, this booklet is divided into certain time periods to identify the particular reasons for these ups and downs.

THE EARLIEST DISCOVERERS AND SETTLERS IN AMERICA

Paleolithic hunters. The first humans to arrive on the American Continent were Paleolithic hunters/gatherers from Siberia who crossed the Bering land bridge between Siberia and Alaska. It is believed that these first humans arrived on American soil about 130, 000 years ago. This belief is based on archeological findings at the Cerutti Mastodon site neat San Diego. Here, archeologists unearthed animal remains, stone anvils, hammer stones and human bone fragments dating back to this time. However, they might not have survived. Later on, other waves of humans crossed the land bridge depending on climatic conditions which made a crossing possible. Again it is believed that the ancestors of the current Native American or Indian population arrived in several major waves between 35,000 and 8,000 years ago. These early arrivals then either stayed in North America or migrated to South America. In both continents, they then split into different tribes.

Vikings. The next explorers were the Vikings in about 1000 CE. Among these early explorers, Erik the Red is best known. He obtained his name from his red hair and beard and founded the first settlement in Greenland which lasted until about 1400. He was the father of Leif Erikson who was the first European to explore the East coast of Canada and founded there a short lived settlement.

Spaniards. The next Europeans who entered our soil were from Spain. Here, of course, Christopher Columbus has to be mentioned who is credited with the discovery of America. Ironically, the new world he discovered was not named after him. The German geographer Martin Waldseemüller accepted the wrong claim by Amerigo Vespucci that he had actually landed on the American mainland before Columbus. Thus in 1507, Waldseemüller published a book in which he named the new land "America". And the name remained until today. There were quite a few Spanish explorers who started to explore the new country looking for gold and silver. However, the Spanish were disappointed and they never found what their colleagues had found in South America. Ponce de Leon explored the coasts of Florida in 1513 and founded a short lived settlement near Fort Meyers, Florida. It was soon attacked by the Indians, de Leon was fatally wounded and the settlement was abandoned. However, he left a long lasting gift behind – a few cows. Having no significant predators, these cows multiplied rapidly and soon were found all over Florida. The latter helped to feed the American soldiers during the Revolutionary War and in particular sustained the meet supply for the Confederate soldiers during the Civil War.

Lucas Vázquez de Ayllón explored the coast between Florida and Delaware and drew the first crude maps of this area. He established San Miguel de Gualdape on October 8, 1526, which became the first Spanish settlement with houses and a church in Florida. It did not last and only 150 out of the original 600 colonists left eventually for home. Hernando de Soto explored the land west of Florida and in 1539 he discovered the Mississippi River. While many attempts to settle in America failed, some succeeded like St. Augustine, Florida. It was founded by Pedro Menendez de Aviles in 1565 and is believed to be the oldest settlement of Spanish origin in the USA. Over the next years, the number of Spanish colonists increased and in 1600 it was about 400,000 for Florida alone which was much larger at this time almost reaching Virginia (1,2)

First English settlers. The next settlers came from England. About 105 colonists left England and reached the Chesapeake Bay on April 26, 1607. The ships moored in the Bay until a suitable place at the James River was found and named the new place Jamestown Colony. This settlement was actually a subsidiary of the Virginia Company of London. The settlers quickly organized themselves in three groups with one group building a fortified wall in a triangular shape, a storage house and some simple houses, the second one planting crops and the third one was to explore the surroundings. The settlement had to be rapidly fortified because the native Indians proved to be more hostile than friendly. Right at the beginning a few hundred Indians attacked the settlement and the attack had to be repulsed with cannon fire from the ship. They would kill colonists who strayed too far away from the colony and also attacked the colony directly several times. In addition to the unfriendly relationship with the Indians, the settlers had to cope with bad water from the river, disease-bearing mosquitoes and limited often spoiled food rations which caused serious health problems like dysentery, severe fevers and finally many of the afflicted settlers died. As a result, the number of settlers dwindled rapidly and only 38 of the about 150 survived the first winter.

A few years later, in September 1620, about 100 English men and women embarked on the ship "Mayflower" to come to the new continent and two months later the ship docked eventually in what is now called Plymouth. Many of them were members of the English Separate Church who had been persecuted or jailed in England for their religious beliefs. They had first moved to the Netherlands to enjoy religious freedom but felt that their customs did not coincide well with their new host country. Thus, they decided to travel to and settle in America. Here, they were referred to as Pilgrims and this title is still used today. Unfortunately, the timing of their arrival was ill chosen and the first winter killed half of the settlers. In the next 3 years, three more ships arrived in the Plymouth Colony. The survivors (at this time called "old comers") and newcomers forged an amiable cooperation with the Indians and build a self-sufficient settlement within the next years. Most memorable is the celebration of the first "Thanksgiving" – a feast with the Pokanoket Indians which lasted three days and included not only food but also playing games and having military exercises (3-11).

In summary, the first permanent settlers from Siberia came in various waves between 35,000 and 8,000 years ago to become the ancestors of today's native Indians. The visits from the Vikings were only transitory. The arrival of the Spanish conquistadors was originally dictated by claiming land for the Spanish crown but also by the urge to find gold and silver. Their first settlements did not survive. The first English settlers coming to found Jamestown were "employees" of an English company and they were here mostly for business reasons albeit later on some stayed here permanently. The first to actually wanted to settle here for good and to make this land to be their new homeland were the English settlers (Pilgrims) in Plymouth.

GERMAN SETTLERS IN AMERICA FROM 1608 TO 1770

Before discussing the immigration of the early German settlers to America, it is necessary to look at the political, religious and socioeconomic conditions of Germany at this time to obtain some clues why some but not other Germans chose to leave their home country for the New World.

Germany 1600 to 1775. During this time span, Germany – or as it better was known as "Das Roemische Reich Deutscher Nation" (The Roman Empire of the German Nation) was a conglomerate of various kingdoms, dukedoms and free cities. Prussia, Saxony, Brandenburg and Bavaria were some of the larger states while some where only a city like the free cities of Augsburg and Cologne. While a German Emperor – or "Kaiser" – was elected by seven electors, he carried little weight and the power rested with the various principalities. In 1500, Germany had a population of about 14 million. This number climbed to about 18 million by 1600.

During this time, two facts have to be mentioned which played a major role in the emigration of German people to America -– the reformation and the misery of the poor people.

Reformation. Religion played a large role in the lives of the German people at this time as signified by the building of the many splendid and massive churches and cathedrals.

The main religion was Roman Catholicism and the church and Pope played a significant role in German politics. Many bishops also were government officials. Such an official was called a "Fuerstbischof" or Prince -Bishop. This, however, changed with the reformation initiated by the teachings of the German monk and theologian Martin Luther (born 1483, Eisleben, Saxony, and died February 18, 1546, in Eisleben). He was not the first who disagreed with the Catholic Church, but he was the first who successfully broke with the Catholic Church by posting and nailing 95 Theses (or points where he disagreed with the church) on the Church door in Wittenberg in 1517 (however, this has never been verified but what is known that he mailed these Theses to his bishop). It was actually a minor event which made him do so. Luther was irritated by the friar Johann Tetzel who preached at this time that sins could be forgiven by purchasing a letter of indulgence with the amount of money depending on the sins committed. After the Theses were made public, he received a number of warnings from the Pope and had to publicly defend his belief. Perhaps the most famous defense was being held in Worms which Luther attended at great risk for his personal well doing and freedom. Here, he ended his dispute with the now famous words: " Hier stehe ich, ich kann nicht anders" (Here I stand, I can do no other). In 1521, he was found guilty, excommunicated and a warrant for his arrest was issued. Also, all his writings and religious ideas were banned. However, he was never apprehended mostly due to the protection provided for him by the Grand Duke and elector Heinrich of Saxony as well as other nobles. Instead he was moved to a castle named Wartburg where he continued to write and promote his religious ideas. It was here that for the first time he translated the entire Bible from Latin into common German which now allowed ordinary people who could read German to study the Holy Scriptures themselves.

From now on, two religions existed, namely Catholicism and Protestantism. The Protestants later split in different groups while all of them agreed on the major beliefs but often disagreed on finer details. Among them, the "Lutheraner" or Lutherans were the most prominent protestantic group. To remain Catholic or become Lutheran was initially determined by the heads of the various states. This was manifested in the phrase: "Cuius regio, eius religio" (Whose realm, his religion). Thus, if a king wanted to remain catholic, all his people had to remain catholic. If a king wanted to become a protestant, then all his people had to follow. This divided Germany in chunks of catholic or protestant areas. Albeit this decree was soon abolished and individual religious choices were allowed. Nevertheless, these effects can still be seen today where Bavaria and the Rhine states are overwhelmingly catholic while the north and east are mostly protestant.

Both religions and their followers strongly believed that their and only their religion was the true religion. This religious intolerance led to severe hardships and misery of many people. Protestants in a catholic area would be suppressed, persecuted or even expelled and the same would happen to Catholics in a protestant area. Fortunately, such suppressed individuals still could relocate into states of their preferred religion. And while these two religions were quite intolerant among each other, they were even more intolerant when it came to some of the small splinter groups of Protestantism like the Mennonites. These followers were severely persecuted and were at the mercy of the state they lived in. This could change if a somewhat tolerant Duke would die and be replaced by a more intolerant one. In fact, they had no save place to live in Germany. This led many of these smaller religious groups to seriously consider leaving Germany and trying to find their freedom elsewhere.

Misery of poor people. At this time, 80% of the people lived in rural areas. The land belonged mostly to a few wealthy land owners and was worked on by "Bauern" (translated as farmers but better known as peasants), These were "Leibeigene" (strictly translated "body owned) or serfs. It was a condition of debt bondage and indentured servitude. Serfs had no personal freedom. They could be bought, sold, or traded within certain restrictions, could be abused with no rights, could not leave the land they were bound to, and could marry only with their lord's permission and often also being forced to paying a wedding tax. In the latter case, nobles could apply the supposed "law" of " jus prima nocte" or the "right of the first night" meaning they could sleep with the bride at the wedding night. The only "right" peasants had, was to work from sunlight to sundown. They were mercilessly exploited by the wealthy and their lives were not much better than those of the American slaves. They lived in shacks and their main foods consisted of bread, potatoes, cabbage and cheese with a very meager sprinkling of meat once in a great while. These miseries led to some revolts and wars between the peasants and nobilities which in German History are called "Bauernkriege" (peasant wars). After some initial successes by the peasants, the final battles were won by the nobilities who had the money and could send trained mercenaries into military actions. In contrast, the peasants had no battle or military experience. After the war, the ring leaders and many peasants were severely punished, tortured and/or executed. The number of peasant casualties has been estimated at 100, 000. Life for the peasants became even more suppressive afterwards. It is interesting that Martin Luther did not support the peasants in their rebellion since he apparently abhorred violence and was more aligned with the bourgeoisie.

In the cities, nobles, merchants and craftsmen (with the latter unified in guilds or unions) could enjoy a good life while again the lower workers were exploited. They also slept in shacks on compacted earth next to dirt, crusted vomit, droppings and rotten food. They also worked long hours. Thus, the lives of these workers – like the serfs - were equally intolerable and miserable.

Thus, rumors about The New World with lots of fertile land which could be obtained and could be worked at as free farmers must have sounded very enticing to some of the more adventurous peasants.

The Thirty Year War. This economic situation became even worth with the Thirty Year War from 1618 to 1648, which had a devastating effect on Germany and its citizens. The war was actually a series of wars fought by various European nations for various reasons including religious, dynastic, territorial, and commercial rivalries. It started when the King of Bohemia, Ferdinand II (who also was Archduke of Austria and King of Hungary) attempted to impose Roman Catholic absolutism on his Bohemian domains. In response, the protestant Nobles from Bohemia rebelled and asked for help from other protestant leaders. At the end, war between these two religious fractions ignited. After many battles, other nations joined the military conflict. One of the first was King Christian IV of Denmark who saw an opportunity to gain valuable territory in Germany. However, he was defeated in 1629. Now Sweden's protestant Gustav Adolf II invaded Germany and with his German protestant partners won many battles until he was mortally wounded. Then the Netherland entered and became briefly involved.

At the end, catholic France entered the war siding with the protestant Swedish. After 30 years, every nation was exhausted and the war stopped with a peace treaty in 1648. The war was a brutal war. For instance, in 1631, imperial troops massacred two-thirds of the population of the City of Magdeburg as punishment to have withstood a siege for too long a time. Each battle fought destroyed many crops and hampered the start of a new farming season. Simultaneously, farm animals were confiscated or killed. All this caused widespread famine mostly afflicting the poor. In addition, many of the mercenaries employed by different armies did not get paid by their "employers" but were told to collect their pay from the "people" they had just occupied. This let them to "collect" their money by plundering, robbing and killing the peasants mercilessly. Germany lay in ashes and people died by the thousands of starvation..

Historians have estimated that between one-fourth and one-third of the German population perished from direct military causes or from illnesses and starvation related to the war. This number was estimated to be 8 million but most likely was much higher.

In summary, it can be surmised that there were two main reasons why people wanted to leave Germany. First, the reformation resulted in a number of new religious beliefs. While Catholics and Lutherans would always find a home somewhere in Germany, members of the smaller denominations were persecuted and often driven from place to place. These people must have longed to find a place somewhere where they could live and pray in peace. Second, life at this time was very difficult, in particular for the poor. They had to live as Serfs with little if any freedom and were always close to starvation. They also must have hoped to one day find a place where they would be free and could farm their own land.

Jamestown. The history of the immigration of German settlers most likely started in 1608, when a second group of settlers arrived at Jamestown and among this group were the first settlers from Germany. This group was also sent by the Virginia Company on the English vessel Mary and Margaret captained by Christopher Newport to Jamestown. They had left England in July 1608 and arrived in Virginia in October of the same year. Of these settlers, eight were of German origin. Five were unnamed glassmakers and three were carpenters or house builders named --Adam, Franz and Samuel. In addition, the records show the arrival of a Swiss German mineral prospector called William Volday. His mission was to find a silver reservoir that was believed to be within the proximity of Jamestown. There was also a Dr Fleischer who was a physician and also held a Doctoral degree in Botany and he was the most educated person in Jamestown at this time. On his tombstone are the following words engraved "Er begutachtete, was der deutsche Boden an Pflanzen hervorbrachte; was in Amerika gedieh, sah er auch und fand dabei den Tod." (He evaluated what plants the German soil produced and he also saw what grew in America and while doing so he died). Again, the old and new settlers faced a bleak future with Indian attacks, diseases and food shortages. During such food shortages, the settlers had to first eat their horses, dogs, and cats— and then turned to eating rats, mice, and shoe leather. In their desperation, some even practiced cannibalism. George Percy, one of the colony's leader, wrote: "And now famine beginning to look ghastly and pale in every face that nothing was spared to maintain life and to do those things which seem incredible, as to dig up dead corpses out of graves and to eat them, and some have licked up the blood which hath fallen from their weak fellows.". The winter of 1609–1610, commonly known as the "Starving Time", took a heavy toll. Of the 500 colonists living in Jamestown in the autumn, less than one-fifth was still alive by March of next year. It is unknown how many of the first German settlers survived or died during this time. By 1620, more Germans settlers had arrived mostly from Hamburg, who again were recruited by the Virginia Company to build and operate one of the first sawmills in the region. However, Captain Thomas Nuce wrote from Virginia in May 1621 that the Germans were facing great difficulties to do so since swift streams required to power the wheels of a sawmill could not be found. In addition, the Germans had great difficulty finding people to help them construct the saw mills. All of the hired German saw mill builders died after a year or so after their arrival. The only surviving son returned to Europe and the German widows were given 27 pounds as compensation. Other skilled German carpenters and soap ash makers did somewhat better and produced some of the colony's first exports of some of their products. Soon, other settlements developed near and further away from Jamestown (10, 18-20).

What is less known (Historic Jamestown Historical Society) is that the colony bought most likely some of the first black people in 1619. According to a letter written by John Rolfe which reads as follows *"About the latter end of August, a Dutch man of War of the burden of a 160 tunes arrived at Point-Comfort, the Comandors name Capt Jope, his Pilott for the West Indies one Mr Marmaduke an Englishman. ... He brought not anything but 20. and odd Negroes, w[hich] the Governo[r] and Cape Merchant bought for victuall[s]."* Victuals meant food. However, the letter refers to a Dutch ship which was actually an English ship. He used this ruse, to shift the blame from an English ship carrying black people to a fictional Dutch ship. Albeit slavery has existed in many parts of the world for hundreds of years, history often sets this event and this year as the beginning of slavery in America. At this time, there lived a few Germans in the colony and it most likely did not concern them a great deal because some of them must have lived as serfs under very similar conditions in Germany.

Another prominent German was Peter Minuit. He was born in Wesel and established himself as a church deacon and diamond cutter. After his marriage, he moved with his family to the Netherlands. There he joined the Dutch West Company and was sent to America as director of the Dutch Colony which stretched from the Delaware to almost Connecticut. Later on, he was approached by the Swedish

King who felt that Sweden was losing out in establishing some claims in the New World to establish a Swedish settlement in America. In 1638, he founded with a group of Swedish settlers a Swedish settlement in the Delaware Bay area. This settlement boasted only a few hundred settlers and lasted only 17 years. Along with bringing Lutheran Christianity to the New World, they were also responsible for introducing the "log cabin". One example located in Gibbstown, New Jersey, dates back to 1638 and is believed the oldest surviving log cabin in America. But Peter Minuit is best known for "buying" the Manhattan Island for the Dutch from the Lenape Native Americans – a piece of land which they actually did not own legally. This area became later the site of the Dutch city of New Amsterdam. Today it is the Borough of Manhattan of New York City. One common account states that Minuit purchased Manhattan Island for $24 worth of trinkets. Another account states he offered beads, cloths and ornaments worth about 60 guilders or about $ 1000 of today's money. Land value of Manhattan is valued today at about 3.5 trillion dollars. Thus, both seem to have won – America got the land very cheap and the Indians got some money for land they never did actually own (21).

Germantown. In 1683, thirteen families or 33 German and German speaking Swiss Quaker and German Mennonite settlers (distinct from the Amish) led by Pastor Franz Pastorius or Francis Daniel Pastorius from Sommerhausen, Franconia, arrived after a 10 week voyage in Philadelphia. They were all Quakers and Mennonites and all had come from Krefeld and Krisheim. Because of their faith, they had been suppressed and persecuted in their homelands and the promise of religious freedom had enticed them to venture to Philadelphia. The names of these families were: Abraham Op den Graeff, Herman Op den Graeff, Dirck Op Den Graeff, Lenart Arets, Jan Seimaens, Willem Streypers, Thones Kunders, Reynier

Tyson, Jan Lucken, Johannes Bleikers, Peter Keurlis, Abraham Tunes and Jan Lensen. Soon after their arrival, they were in for a major disappointment because the land which had been promised to them was unavailable. Thus, they had to settle for some less desirable land which they purchased. Quickly, they marked off land lots for the families which were later assigned by lottery. Soon after, they started to make available caves more habitable and to actually build small houses. Thus, "Deutschestaedel" (Germantown) next to Philadelphia was established. Nevertheless, life in the new country was difficult for the first two winters. Low in provisions and money, the settlers had to exist mainly on what game and fish they could find. And as expected, a fair number of these settlers did not survive the first winter. Conditions improved after the second winter, however, and the tiny colony was strengthened by the arrival of further immigrants from Germany. Now settlers came not only from Krefeld and Krisheim but also from Palatinate, Alsace, Swabia, Saxony and Switzerland. In 1689, the settlement received a charter from William Penn validated by the English King to establish its own government. The government consisted of the bailiff, four burgesses and six committeemen. They could enact their own laws, levy fines and assess taxes. This charter was in effect until 1707. During these early times, Mennonites and Quakers worshipped together in the homes of Tunes Kunders and in 1690, they chose William Rittenhouse to be their minister (a small park in Philadelphia still bears his name). In 1708, the first Mennonite meeting house in the New World was built on land which Arnold von Vossen had supplied. The settlement grew rapidly and at the time of the Revolutionary War it numbered close to 100,000 Germans.

Pastorius wrote to his father justifying his move to Ameriva "Die Ungezügeltheit und Sünden der europäischen Welt nehmen ständig in einer Weise zu, dass ein gerechtes Gottesurteil nicht mehr lange ausbleiben kann. So übergebe ich mich der besonderen Führung des Allerhöchsten, nach Pennsylvania zu reisen. Hier sollte es möglich sein, in neuem Land ein stilles und christliches Leben zu führen.'(" The naughtiness and sins in the European world increase gradually in such a manner so that a judgment by God must come soon. Thus I submit myself to the lead of the Lord to travel to Pennsylvania. Here it will be possible in a new land to experience a quiet and Christian life") About the beginning of their new life, he wrote " Es ist alles nur Wald und Gestrüpp. Arbeitsleut' und Bauern sind hier ernstlich am nötigsten, und wünsche ich mir ein Dutzend starke Tiroler, die dicken Eichenbäume niederzuwerfen.". (It is all only forest and scrub . Workers and farmers are seriously needed and I wish I had a dozen of strong Bavarians to knock down the big Oak trees"). He was a proliferate writer and his book "beehive" is now in the University of Pennsylvania's rare book room. It contains poetry, his thoughts on religion and politics, and lists of books he consulted along with excerpts from those books. Also of interest is his geographical description of Pennsylvania, first published under the title " Umständige geographische Beschreibung der allerletzt erfundenen Provintz Pennsylvania" (General geographic description of the lastly discovered province Pennsylvania). In 1688, he and three Germantown Quakers joined in signing the "The 1688 Germantown Quaker Petition Against Slavery" which is the first petition against slavery made in the English colonies. In 1697, the first paper mill and print shop were established in Germantown and in 1732 the first German-language newspaper," Philadelphische Zeitung" (Philadelphian News Paper), was published in the United States. In 1764, The German Society of Pennsylvania was founded and it is still serving the Philadelphia community, providing lectures, discussions, fun events and more. It has an excellent library with many old books in German (22-26).

Amish. Next, other religious groups came to the USA most notably the Amish. There is not much difference between the Mennonites and Amish except the Amish eschew most modern technology and practice "shunning" which is a form of social isolation of members not attending church or leaving the faith. Even today, old school Amish people prefer horse and buggy as their transportation.

The first Amish settlers arrived in the USA around 1720 and continued until 1740. Most of these early and later settlers came from German speaking areas of Switzerland and southern Germany. Originally, Switzerland was quite repressive to the Amish so that many Amish had moved to Southern Germany like the Pfalz (area between the Rhine and vogues mountains) Elsass and Bavaria. They arrived in large and small groups. One of the larger groups originating from the Pfalz (area between the Rhine and the Alsatian Vogues) consisted of 500 people. They came single or as families. Often families were of considerable size. One ship's record lists, for instance, " MILDER, Christer, MILDER, Josephine, MILDER, Hans Adam, MILDER, Hans Jerig, MILDER, Hieronimus, MILDER, Jacob, MILDER, Greta". The first settlers settled nearby Philadelphia in a community which they named Northkill settlement. The name was derived from a local creek and existing fort. At its peak, the community may have had up to 200 residents. It was, however, short lived .In 1757 (there is some disagreement on the exact date), one of the settlers by the name of Jacob Hochstetler and his family came under attack by the Delaware Indians. Apparently true to their peaceful faith, Jacob restrained his boys from firing their rifles. Unfortunately, these peaceful gestures were not reciprocated by the Indians who killed his wife, a daughter and a son. In 1757.the settlement was abandoned.

At this place, a marker was erected which still stands today and reads: "NORTHKILL AMISH--- The first organized Amish

Mennonite congregation in America. Established by 1740. Disbanded following Indian attack. September 29,1757, in which a provincial soldier and three members of the Jocob Hochstetter family were killed near this point."

During this time, other Amish settlements were also established with the one in Lancaster, Pennsylvania being the oldest and one which is still in existence. Such other settlements can now be found in 28 states like Indiana and Ohio as well as Canada. The Amish now number approximately 250,000 today. Most Old Order Amish speak Pennsylvania "Dutch". Pennsylvania Dutch originally derived from the word "Deitsch" (dialect of the word German). Most Amish today speak both Dutch and English but Dutch still dominates in the house and in Church while English is used in schools, business transactions and other outside encounters. One saying goes like this: "Bisli Deitsh gayt en langa vayk (A little Deutch goes a long way). A common Pennsylvania song is *"Mei Vadder un Mudder sinn Deitsch"* (My father and mother are German). Among the many innervations from these Amish settlers, the Conestoga wagon is the most prominent. This wagon was named after the Conestoga Indians. Conestoga wagons have distinctive curved floors and canvas covers arched over wooden hoops. They were drawn by oxen or horses and could deliver large amounts of agricultural farm products. They became very popular and wide spread and soon carried diverse products from state to state (27-31).

There were a number of other religious groups from Germany albeit much smaller which also settled in this country at these times. They included the Neue Taufer or Baptist Dunkers, Schwenkfelders, Waldensians and Moravians. It is perhaps surprising to learn in how many groups the Protestants splintered just to follow different charismatic preachers and to accommodate some diverse beliefs.

The Neue Taufer. This faith originated in 1708 near the village of Schwarzenau, Germany, along the Eder River. Outsiders called them "dunkers" because they fully immersed or "dunked" their baptismal candidates three times in nearby streams. They established many settlements and congregations throughout Pennsylvania, New Jersey, Maryland, Virginia, and the Carolinas. In the early 1700, Antietam was the largest congregation with hundreds of members, stretching over vast territory in south-central Pennsylvania and north-central Maryland. Gradually, these Brethren sub-divided. Presently, there are seven denominations that can be traced back to this original group from Schwarzenau.

Schwenkfelders. The Schwenkfelders were followers of Caspar Schwenckfeld von Ossig (1489-1561), a German Reformer. The faith believes that the Bible is not a "paper pope" but mere words that require God's Spirit to bring them to life. The church also places emphasis on the inner workings of the Holy Spirit to create a new person. Interestingly, the earliest followers in the 16th century were intellectual, professional women (a rare breed at the time). The first of the Schwenkfelders arrived in Philadelphia on September 22, 1734. The 15-year-old Christopher Schultz documented the voyage in his journal. This is the only written record of an Atlantic crossing at the time. Since they could not acquire a large enough piece of land for their settlement, each family started its homestead separately ranging from Chestnut Hill, near Philadelphia, into what are now Berks and Lehigh counties. All followers of this faith did leave Germany and other countries and the only Schwenkfelders are now found in the USA.

Waldenserians. The Waldenserians or Waldensians were basically formed by Peter Waldo (1140?-1206 or 07), a wealthy merchant of Lyons, who became convinced in 1173 that every man had a right to read and interpret the Scriptures for himself (which is way before Martin Luther expressed the same belief). He then personally followed Christ's admonition to the rich and sold all his goods and distributed the proceeds among the poor. He made some provisions for the support of his family and then went forth to preach as he felt the Lord wanted him to do as a poor man. His followers soon numbered in the thousands and spread to other countries including Germany. Many Waldenserians, having escaped persecution in their homelands by making their way to the tolerant Dutch Republic, crossed the Atlantic to start anew in the New Netherland colony and established the first church in North America on Staten Island in 1670.

Moravians. The Moravian Church was started by a Catholic priest named Jan Hus (in English John Hus) in the early fifteenth century. Hus wanted the Church to return what early Christianity did namely performing the liturgy in the language of the people and allowing lay people to receive both the bread and the cup during communion. For this he was burnt at the stake. His followers fled from Moravia to Germany. Thus, they named themselves Moravians. In Germany they took up residence in a town known as Herrnhut. They were protected by Nicholas Ludwig von Zinzendorf, a pietistic nobleman from Saxony, Germany. The Moravian Church firsts attempts to establish a settlement in America began in 1735 in Georgia. Unfortunately, their attempt was unsuccessful and the Moravian Church moved its community to Pennsylvania in 1741. Here, they purchased land from the estate of George Whitefield and established a settlement of Bethlehem, Pennsylvania, which became the center of Moravian activity in colonial America. Even today, there exists a Moravian College which is a private liberal arts college in Bethlehem, Pennsylvania, offering undergraduate and graduate degrees. Founded in 1851, it is one of the oldest higher educational institutions in the USA. Other Moravian congregations began to take up residence also in other parts of Pennsylvania as well as New Jersey and Maryland. In 1753, a Moravian congregation purchased land in North Carolina and called it Wachovia. This later on became the city of Winston-Salem (32-38).

Voyage. What is frequently not mentioned in the lives of these early settlers is the voyage from their home country to America. These voyages lasted from 2 - 4 months and could be smooth or quite stormy. They were not only dangerous due to the fact that many of these ships were old and in dire need of repair but passengers had to endure extreme hardships sometimes ending in death. Right from the start, passengers found out that they had to live in overcrowded conditions. Most were housed in the lower decks and seldom saw daylight. They had to live among packages, boxes, storage cases and other objects with little more space than their body's width. They also had to share their spaces with lice, rats and mice. The food was rationed and mostly salty and the water was often foul in particular at the end of the voyage. They were constantly shaken by the rocking of the vessel which was more or less depending on the weather but always present. One of those who made the voyage, a Gottlieb Mittelberg, a schoolmaster, wrote ".......during the voyage there is on board these ships terrible misery, stench, fumes, horror, vomiting, many kinds of seasickness, fever, dysentery, headache, heat, constipation, boils, scurvy, cancer, mouth rot, and the like, all of which come from old and sharply-salted food and meat, also from very bad and foul water, so that many die miserably". Another diary records "It was a severely harsh trip on filthy ships which were hardly seaworthy and with passengers packed 'like herrings' and exposed to rats, disease, thirst, and starvation. Their provisions fell short, and in the last eight weeks they had no bread; but a pint of grouts [crushed oats] was all the allowance for five persons per day. They all ate rats and mice they could catch. The price of a rat was 18 pence, a mouse was 6 pence, and water 6 pence a quart --------Parents must often watch their offspring suffer miserably, die, and be thrown into the ocean --------One day, just as we had a heavy gale, a woman on our ship, who was to give birth and could not under the circumstances of the storm, was pushed through the porthole and dropped into the sea, because she was far in the rear of the ship and could not be brought forward". Thus, the voyage lasting for months to the new country was often the most unpleasant and dangerous part of the entire adventure (39-46).

William Penn. It is perhaps surprising that all these religious groups landed in Philadelphia and established their communities in or nearby Philadelphia. The reason for this was William Penn (1644 – 1718). Penn was an established lawyer and prominent Quaker in England. William's father had died in 1670. Part of William's inheritance was a crown debt of £16,000 which his father had lent to Charles II soon after the monarchy was re-established. In 1681, in settlement of this debt, the king granted land to William Penn on the west bank of the Delaware River in the American Colonies. Penn wanted to name this colony Sylvania, but the King insisted on the name Penn being prefixed in memory of his father - so it became Pennsylvania. William Penn then visited his new colony in 1682 and spent two years there improving the conditions of the new colony. In order to attract new settlers and workers, he and other Quakers left Philadelphia and traveled to and through Germany praising the virtues of the fledgling colony. In particular, its religious freedom and the availability to easily obtain land parcels with fertile soil were emphasized. Penn's words and promises were well received and spread rapidly soon all over Germany. The promise of religious freedom was particularly well received by the various suppressed minority faiths and the open land with fertile soil was an incentive to the poor farmers. Here, in America some could finally find religious freedom while other could obtain land and farm it as free men (47)

Other settlers. During this time, most historical attention is usually being paid to these early religious settlers and their settlements because they left many records about their early lives in the New World. Some attention is also paid to individual settlers who achieved some importance or success during their early stays in America. But hundreds and thousands of individuals who came to America, blended unnoticed into every day's life and disappeared from history because they did not achieve some immediate importance or left any official records. These individuals were mostly of the poorer classes and most did not come for religious reasons but to escape their dreadful and miserable existence in Germany. This was exemplified by the words of Heinrich Melchior Muehlenberg, who was born in Einbeck in Braunschweig-Lüneburg and later immigrated in 1742 to this country and became an important church patriarch: "However, there were many more immigrants who came for economic reasons to escape dire economic conditions and bondage in their homeland and to improve the fortunes of their own lives".

However, some of these almost forgotten individuals and families who did not achieve some importance during their lifetimes still contributed to the well being and success of the United States albeit in an unintentional way. The following is one example: In 1741, Hans Nicolas Eisenhauer and his family emigrated from Karlsruhe, Hessen, to America and settled first in Lancaster, Pennsylvania. Later on, the family moved to Abilene, Kansas. They changed the name Eisenhauer (literally translated as "iron beater" or meaning an iron worker) into the way "hauer" would be pronounced as "hower" and called themselves Eisenhower. Their son Frederick would marry Anna Margaret Dissinger, who was born in Gersweiler, Nassau-Saarbrucken, before coming to America. At about the same time, John Adam Matter with wife Anna Catherine moved from Germany to America in 1751. A few decades later, members of The Eisenhower and Matter families would meet and Jacob Frederick Eisenhower would marry Rebecca Matter. Their son David Jacob would then marry Ida Elizabeth Stover. Up to now, these families were almost forgotten. However, their son named Dwight D. Eisenhower changed everything. He later served as Supreme Allied Commander in Europe during World War II, and as two terms President of the United States. If it would not have been for these early German immigrants, there would not have been a Dwight D. Eisenhower. There must be quite a number of similar stories where the early lives of German immigrants gave rise to important individuals later on who contributed significantly to the well being and success of the Unites States of America.

Early hardships for the poor. However, the arrival of the poorer immigrants did not immediately bring freedom but in many cases brought similar hardships as indentured servants. At this time you could either pay for your voyage or do not pay and work your fare off later on in America. For instance, when a ship arrived, paid passengers could leave the ship immediately, while unpaid passengers had to wait. Wealthy Philadelphian citizens who needed servants would go on board and select individuals they felt suitable for their needs and would pay the fare to the captain. This would bind or indenture the chosen individual to the payer for 3-7 years. Young people, from ten to fifteen years of age, had to serve until they were twenty-one years old.

Sometimes husband and wife were sold separately or parents had to sell their children. In some ways, this was like the lifes of the slaves albeit shorter. All this was legal and documented. This could mean that families might not see each other for many years and sometimes never. This indentured time depending on the master could be hard work or could be tolerable.

Unfortunately, it was mostly brutal and cruel and many of the indentured servants would die during this time. Whipping was an accepted way of punishment and it was applied freely on the bare back of the individual. Life was particularly cruel for women who often were abused by their masters. And little could be done because indentured servants had few if any rights. It was also almost impossible to run away because such individuals would be quickly apprehended since the people who would detain or return a "deserter" would receive a very handsome reward. After capture, the indentured time would be increased depending on how long he or she had escaped. At the end of the term, the servant might be given clothes, tools, a small sum of money, or even a piece of land. During these early times, 50-75% of all poor German immigrants were indentured servants. Nevertheless, the ones who survived this ordeal obtained long expected freedom for the rest of their lives and could now use all their efforts to achieve their dreams. And indeed many did and with their work and inventions moved America into the future (48-50, 156).

Challenges at arrival. The first challenge presented itself as the settlers were getting their first glance of Philadelphia. They saw a city with about 10, 000 to 20, 000 residents depending on the time at their arrivals and they saw a city with streets which were at strict right angles interspersed with little parks. This was quite different from what they were used to, namely villages and towns where streets would meander criss-cross at various angles.

The next challenge was the language since few Germans spoke English. Thus, it must have been quite frightening to the new arrivals to hear all these people speak with no word to be understood. It was quite comforting when German speaking citizens came to them and they could ask questions or obtain information. Like always, most of these German speaking residents were well-meaning and quite helpful. There were always a few who unfortunately exploited the newcomers. Thus, it follows that these early Germans – like other nationalities – would try to move together and to congregate in German speaking neighborhoods with their well known German shops and bars. Interestingly, many of these neighborhoods continued to exist well into the 20th century. When the author arrived in Chicago in 1961, he could easily find the typical German neighborhood where he could order in German all the typical German food specialties like "Blutwurst" (blood sausage) or "Leberkaes" (liver cheese). He would visit a German bar and restaurant where a beautifully carved wooden board from 1788 displayed the following words "Drinkst Du, stirbst Du -- Drinkst Du nicht, stirbst Du auch – also drink)" (If you drink, you will die – If you do not drink, you will also die – Thus, drink). Soon German news papers were published with "Die Philadelphische Zeitung" (The Philadelphian News Paper) published by nobody else but Benjamin Franklin. This was followed by many others like "Germantauner" Zeitung" (Germantown Paper) and "Die New Yorker Staatszeitung" (NY state newspaper). It has been claimed that by 1890, there were over 1,000 German language newspapers being published in the United States. After this time, this number declined rapidly in part due the World War I and the emergence of the Third Reich in Germany.

Up to 1800, German was the second most widely spoken language in the U.S.A. As a matter of fact the first Bible was printed in America in German before it was printed in English. It was even said at one time that officials considered to make German the official language. It is often said that such a resolution was voted on in congress but ended up in a tie with a German speaking member voting against the German language. While this sounds interesting it is not quite true. However, in 1795 congress considered a proposal to print federal laws in both English and German. This proposal failed by only 1 vote. English remained the official language in legal matters and in public use. This did not mean that German was now abandoned but it continued and was often the first language children learned in larger German communities. The two daughters of the author grew up with German as their first language until they started to mingle with other children in the neighborhood. This was the time when they began to speak English. It was quite amusing in the beginning when our children would speak German and the other children English – and they got along well. Our daughters later on would use it as a "secret" language to quickly communicate with each other and without the others understanding what was being said (51).

Another challenge occurred if individuals would get sick. There were few German physicians to go to and most settlers did not understand English physicians or did not trust them. But this mattered little since physicians at these times were usually ill educated and were of little or no help but in many instances actually caused more harm than good to the patient. They used mainly blood-letting often draining one fourth to one half of all the body's blood from their patients. Laxatives were routinely prescribed and the medications contained often arsenic and mercury. Thus, our early ancestors were left mostly with their folks remedies. Plants frequently used were chamomile, thyme, sage, licorice roots and oregano. Flowers were sometimes used based on the shape of their leaves or blossoms. A kidney shaped blossom or leaf was good for kidney problems while heart shaped ones helped the ailing heart. While these remedies were most likely of no help, they at least did no harm. Religion also played a significant role in that diseases and plaques were believed to be sent be God as punishment for worldly sins. Praying and self punishments were then employed to get rid of them. Taking advantage of the medical plight which the settlers faced, some enterprising physicians exploited this situation and wrote a number of "self-help-books". Some of which can be found in the Library of the German Society of Pennsylvania in Philadelphia. Some of these recipes are indeed very strange to our present understanding of medicine. One of the books shown below is the "Drecksapotheke" (Dirt pharmacy). Here. it is recommended that ailing eyes can be helped with the feces of a falcon: "Des Falckenkoths Krafft vor die AugenKrankheiten bekraeffigt D. Reinerus Solenander, indem er schreibt, er hatte vor die Bloedigkeit des Gesichtes allemahl sonderlich wohl befunden folgendes Pulver. Dazu er nimmt gedoerten Falckenkoth 1 Quintlein, Fenchelsamen. 1 Loth. Beides pulverisirt ergal subtil und thut alle Morgen etwas wenigs davon in die Augenwinckel" (The power of the Falcon's feces recommends D Reinerus Solenander.for the stupidity of the face and advices the following well received powder. One takes the well dried feces of the falcon 1 Quint, Fennel seeds 1 Lot. Both should be well pulverized and should be applied a bit every morning to the angles of the eyes). Looking at these medical conditions and remedies, it is easy to understand that the death rate was very high and the life expectancy low. The latter was estimated to be about 35 years. This includes, however, the high infant mortality – estimated that only 50% of infants would survive their first year -so that the life expectancy of surviving adults might have been somewhat higher (52-56).

Die "Dreck.Apotheke"(The Dirt Pharmacy) – later edition (Google)

In summary, many of the Settlers of which we have written records at this time span, came for religious reasons and most were members of certain German minority religions other than Catholics or Protestants. They all left because of religious intolerance and persecution in their home country seeking religious freedom in the "New World" which indeed they found. Interestingly, while remnants of some of these minority groups still exist in America today, they have completely disappeared in Germany. However, there were also many poor who left Germany because they were exploited and their lives were miserable. If they could have paid for their voyage, they could start immediately to find work or obtain land to be worked on. If they could not have paid for their voyage they would most likely have been indentured and their misery would continue for some time before they were free to start a new life. These early settlers faced many challenges starting with the voyage which most likely was the most miserable and dangerous part of their adventure. At arrival, they faced a different culture with a different language and little medical help except what they practiced themselves. In addition, food shortage and cold winters added to their problems. Thus, the new life in America started with many hardships which even led to the death of quite a few of these courageous people.

THE WAR OF INDEPENDENCE

The next waves of German people entering this country was during and after the War of Independence albeit many of them did do so involuntarily.

The War of Independence. Decades before the war, tensions had been growing between the American Colonists and the English King and British Parliament. This led to many skirmishes like the Boston massacre where British soldiers opened fire on a group of Colonists and the Boston Tea Party where colonists dressed as Mohawk Indians dumped chests of tea into Boston Bay.

While many colonists supported these actions, others did not. At this time, the country was divided into loyalists who sided with the British and wanted no major changes and the Patriots which were against the British and wanted independence. It has been estimated that patriots made up about 70% while loyalists accounted for 15-20% with the rest being neutral or "fence sitters".

Thus, some colonial delegates met in Philadelphia in 1774 and formed The First Colonial Congress which condemned taxation without representation and demanded certain rights including liberty and right to a just trial from the British Parliament.

However, on April 18, 1775, British troops marched from Boston to nearby Concord, Massachusetts, to seize a cache of weapons. As is well know, Paul Revere and other riders sounded the alarm and colonial militiamen began to fire on the British soldiers. Thus, the Battles of Lexington and Concord marked the beginning of the War of Independence or Revolutionary War. While war already had started, The Continental Congress voted in 1776 to adopt officially the Declaration of Independence. In response, the British sent a bit over 30, 000 soldiers to America to crush the rebellion.

Of interest is to read the early Army enlistment agreement which says that the Continental Army initially expected recruits to provide their own arms and accoutrements. Recruits in Massachusetts who signed this agreement to enlist for the duration of the war declared that "each of Us do engage to furnish and carry with us into the Service, a good effective Fire-Arm, and also a Bayonet (if to be obtained) Cartridge-Box and Knap-Sack ; and if no Bayonet, in Lieu thereof, a Sword, Hatchet or Tomahawk." The main weapon was the musket firing round lead balls. These balls when fired rapidly started to drop towards the earth. To make matters worse, it had no sights. To demonstrate its inaccuracy, it has been claimed that the colonists at the battle of Lexington/Concord fired over 10 000 shots to kill and wound about 250 British soldiers.

After the declaration, there were a number of minor and major battles fought. In many cases, soldiers of each side would march towards each other and stop when about 50 yards apart. Then they would shoot. Afterwards they would try to reload their muskets as fast as possible.. In the beginning, most battles were won by the British. The war did not look good for the colonists and many felt that the war was lost. But the colonists with the help from the French did not give up and finally succeeded in the battle of Yorktown. Here in 1781, the British faced the colonists enforced by French soldiers on land while the French fleet blocked the British from receiving supplies and prevented them from escaping. The British surrendered. After this battle, a number of minor battles were still fought but finally American and British negotiators met in Paris on September 3, 1783 and Great Britain formally recognized the independence of the United States in the Treaty of Paris.

Independence was won, but at the cost of many human lives. Total American battle casualties in the Revolutionary War were about 7,000. Civilian casualties were estimated to be 1,000. About 8,000 died in British prisons and about 10,000 died of various diseases. Interestingly, more soldiers died of diseases than in military actions. In addition, there were about 8,000 wounded and being more or less crippled for life. The exact number of German Americans or German immigrants who died or was crippled during this war is not known.

Total number of British army casualties from battle and diseases in the Revolutionary War has been estimated to have been about 24,000. Again, more British soldiers were killed by diseases than during military actions.

Germans fighting for independence. The people who wanted independence and were willing to fight for it included many German-Americans and freshly immigrated Germans. While many of these Germans fought side by side with soldiers from all kinds of ethnic backgrounds, some units of the colonial Army were exclusively created to consist of ethnic Germans only. In 1776, the Second Continental Congress authorized the formation of the 8th Maryland Regiment (or the German Battalion or German Regiment) to consist only of colonial ethnic Germans with German as the official military language..The commander was a German immigrant by the name of Nicholas Haussegger. At the same time, Pennsylvania Germans were specifically recruited for the American Provost Corps under the command of Captain Bartholomew von Heer who was a born Prussian and who had immigrated to Reading, Pennsylvania prior to the war. This Corps was used to gather intelligence, enforce security, supervise prisoner of war operations and in some instances to fight in battle. They were also responsible to guard Washington's headquarters during the Battle of Yorktown. The Corps can be considered a predecessor of the current United States Military Police. They were not well liked by other units of the Colonial Army because of their police like duties and because they spoke German and hardly any English (61).

What also has to be mentioned is that many Germans fought the war under the French flag. These were Germans who previously had enlisted in the French army in France and were now being shipped to America. These were eight German speaking regiments numbering about 2,500 men. They were commanded by Johann de Kalb who was born in Bavaria. He was wounded in battle and died in America (61).

Of all the Germans who fought in the colonial army, Friedrich von Steuben is most likely the best known immigrant. He was born in 1730 in Magdeburg, Saxony and joined the Prussian army at the age of 16. Here, he rose to the rank of lieutenant and learned the military discipline that made the Prussian army the best in Europe. Then he was dismissed for unknown reason and bounced from job to job and was always looking for a new opportunity. He sensed it when the war in America started. In September 1777, he decided to join the Continental Army with a recommendation letter from Benjamin Franklin. With this letter, he sailed to America to join George Washington (albeit the letter claimed falsely that he had been a lieutenant general). George Washington made him Inspector General and instructed him to turn his troops into real soldiers. This was no easy undertaking because at this time all he had to work with was an undisciplined army. He found soldiers without uniforms, carrying rusted muskets, missing bayonets and companies with men missing and unaccounted for. Short enlistments meant constant turnover and little order with regiment sizes varying wildly. Thus, von Steuben used Prussian army drills and applied them vigorously to the soldiers. He taught them how to reload their muskets quickly after firing, how to charge with a bayonet and how to march and fight in compact columns instead of groups of different sizes. This must have been quite a contrast, von Steuben in his elaborate and splendid uniform and the soldiers in their dirty and torn uniforms. At the same time, he wrote detailed lists to the officers what to do and how to handle their subordinates. He also gave them more responsibilities to take care of their troops. During these drills - it is said- he often raged in German and poor French and English.

He also made sure that the troops would be properly dressed and fed. During all these drills he began to understand his soldiers and the soldiers began to appreciate this foreign noble man. He once wrote "You say to your soldier 'Do this and he doeth it'; but I am also obliged to say: 'This is the reason why you ought to do that: and then he does it better.'" His drills and tactics soon proved very successful and the Continental Army became more successful and eventually went on to win more battles due to military drills by this German noble man

After the war the governor of New York granted von Steuben a large estate in the Mohawk Valley where he died in 1794. As a sideline, he was also homosexual which most likely contributed to his job problems in Germany (61).

There were, of course, quite a number of other Germans who joined the Colonial Army. One of these immigrants was Friedrich Heinrich Freiherr von Weissenfels. He was born in Prussia and served in the Prussian army and other armies before coming to America. Here, he joined the Army as an officer due to the authorization of the British Parliament which allowed for "a certain number of foreign Protestants, who have served abroad as officers or engineers, to act and rank as officers or engineers in the British army in America...".

About fifty officers' commissions were given to immigrated Germans and one of these was awarded to von Weissenfels. Although he had taken an Oath of Allegiance to Great Britain, he lrft the British Army and joined the Colonial Army much to the chagrin of his family since his sister wrote: "Following his principles rather than the advice of friends, he early joined the side of the revolutionaries in the American Revolutionary War." (62).

Another German immigrant, albeit less well known, contributed largely to the wellbeing and success of the Colonial Army. His name was Christopher Ludwick, the Gingerbread man. Christopher Ludwig (sometimes spelled Ludwick) was born into a baker family at Giessen, Hesse-Darmstadt, Germany in 1720. After receiving a limited education, he learned to be a baker. Among all the cakes he baked, he specialized in making Gingerbread. Gingerbread is a baked good consisting of flour, ginger, cloves, nutmeg or cinnamon and sweetened with honey, sugar or molasses. The dough is then pressed in molds which transfer different shapes, figures or flowers onto the gingerbread.

In 1754, he went **to** Philadelphia to set up his own business which did very well. Soon, he owned 9 houses and a farm near Germantown. As a wealthy merchant, he was elected to the local government. When money was needed for the war, he said at one of the local meetings in broken English "Mr. President, I am but a poor gingerbread baker, but put my name down for two hundred pounds". In 1776, he entered the army and one of his assignments was to visit a camp of Hessian soldiers to persuade them to desert. Indeed, he was partially successful in that some deserted and joined the colonial army. In 1777 he was appointed Baker – General for the army according to ""Resolved, That Christopher Ludwick be, and is hereby appointed Superintendent of Bakers and Director of Baking in the army of the United States ; and that he shall have power to engage, and by permission of the Commander-in-Chief, or officer commanding at any principal post, all persons to be employed in his business, and to regulate their pay, making proper report of his proceedings, and using his best endeavors to rectify all abuses in the article of bread". As Baker-General he said:" I do not wish to grow rich by the war. I have money enough. I will furnish one hundred and thirty-five pounds of bread for every hundred pounds of flour you put into my hands." While this sounds very generous, it has to be recognized that the addition of water to the flour to make the dough increased its weight so that he did not lose but actually might have gained a bit. Nevertheless, his contributions of good bread instead of the customary bad bread helped to feed many hungry soldiers. After the war, he settled at his farm. During the yellow-fever epidemic in 1798, he distributed bread free of charge to the poor. In 1801, he died in Philadelphia (63).

In addition and little mentioned in the literature are the contributions and sacrifices of the women. These women whose husbands served in the army had to take care at home of the fields and animals to supply the army with food or to sew uniforms to cloth the soldiers. But many actually travelled with their husbands as "camp followers" estimated to be sometimes close to 10,000. Here they often supplied water to the soldiers during and after battle like the legendary "Molly Pitcher" and they cared for the wounded. Some actually fought like Margaret Corbin who "manned" a cannon when her husband was mortally wounded. Among these women but lost in archives or forgotten there must have been also many German women and women of German descent (64).

Germans refusing to fight for independence. There were a number of German-Americans who wanted to fight for independence but they were prohibited from doing so mainly based on their religious beliefs. These were members of certain religious groups like the Amish, Quakers, Mennonites or Brethren who believed in diplomacy peace and they rejected any forms of physical violence in particular war. Their belief is based on the words of Jesus:" Ye have heard that it hath been said: an eye for an eye and a tooth for a tooth: but I say unto you, that ye resist not evil: but whosoever shall smite thee on thy right cheek, turn to him the other also". They all believed that this teaching of Jesus did not merely apply to personal physical conflict but also applied to times of war as well. To make matters worse, many had signed at their arrival allegiance to the English Crown which many were not willing to break.

Nevertheless, in spite of their religious beliefs and previous oath of alliance with England, a small number joined the army in direct opposition to their faith. These people often considered the Revolution to be a fight for a divinely-ordained new system of government that would change the world for the better and they formed the society of Free Quakers. Due to their action, they were expelled from the original churches.

Most, however, followed their religious beliefs and stayed home. They soon found out that they were socially attacked, called cowards and traitors and were shunned by neighbors whose family members were fighting in the war. To make matters worse, they were soon required by various state and local governments to sign an oath of allegiance which, for instance, in Pennsylvania was worded like "I do swear (or affirm) that I renounce and refuse all allegiance to George III, King of Great Britain, his heirs and successors; and that I will be faithful and bear true allegiance to the Commonwealth of Pennsylvania as a free and independent State, and that I will not at any time, do or cause to be done any matter or thing that will be prejudicial, or injurious to the freedom and independence thereof;...." This, again, went against their religious beliefs since they believed that Jesus had forbidden the swearing of any oath. Even if there was a provision (--or affirm), they still felt it to be like an oath. Thus, most objectors refused to sign this document. However, all individuals refusing to sign were soon stripped of certain rights like not serving on juries, suing for debts, or buying or selling lands. Furthermore, their travels were restricted and violations could be punished by imprisonment. Eventually, taxes were levied against them and their properties were confiscated if these taxes could not be paid. As a result, these individuals suffered great personal and economic hardships and losses by adhering steadfastly to their religious beliefs.

Germans fighting for the English Crown. Before the war, a minority of the colonists were loyal to the British Crown. As is human nature, they were quickly abused and persecuted and were publicly dunked in lakes, hung from poles, or tarred and feathered by angry mobs. In spite, many of them remained loyal even after outbreak of the war and a fair number of them joined the British army while some fled to safety in Canada.

The English army itself was comprised of English soldiers, colonists and hired German soldiers.

It was a formidable army with most soldiers being well trained and battle hardened. Their only weakness was that they had to fight in a distant land and depended heavily on its supply from England. This problem became even worse with the entry of France into the war which with their ships blocked many of the English supply vessels from reaching their destination. The number of colonists or Tory soldier has been estimated to have been about 9000. The number of English soldiers was about 20,000.

Another group consisted of soldiers who came from Germany. These were not volunteers but were "rented" to England to fight its war. At this time, Germany was still a conglomerate of a number of larger and smaller principalities governed by kings, archdukes, dukes and other lesser nobilities. The sovereigns of these states were always in need of money. Thus, they decided to "rent" part of their army to others and let their soldiers fight their wars. This was common practice during these times and it was a lucrative business since there was always a war going on in Europe. Thus, in 1776 England formed a treaty with several German states that allowed it to hire their soldiers. This was cheaper for England and brought needed money to the German sovereigns. Of course, the soldiers were never asked. These soldiers came mostly from Hessen but smaller contingents came from Brunswick-Wolfenbuettel, Ansbach Bayreuth, Waldeck Hannover and Anhalt-Zerbst. These soldiers were generally referred to as "Hessians". However, they were no "mercenaries" as sometimes referred to since they did not voluntarily join the army. They are more proper called "auxiliary" troops since they were sent by a sovereign often against their own will. They would fight as strictly German units but were sometimes intermingled with the English soldiers. The British common soldiers distrusted the primarily German-speaking colonists and Hessians and often treated them with contempt. Finally, General Howe, the supreme commander, ordered that "the English should treat the Germans as brothers." This order only became effective when the Germans had learned to stammer a little English. Apparently, this was a prerequisite for the English to show them any affection. At the height of the war, there were about 30 000 auxiliary soldiers in America. These soldiers fought a brutal war in the beginning in that they did not take prisoners or if prisoners were taken they would execute them later. They did not consider the colonial soldiers "soldiers" but rebels. Based partially on the practice of the Colonial Army who respected the life of the prisoners, they later changed their barbaric ways. One English commander wrote: "Our Hessians and our brave Highlanders gave no quarter and it was a fine sight to see with what alacrity they dispatched the rebels with their bayonets, after we surrounded them so they could not resist." Although exact figures are difficult to obtain, about 2,000 died in battle, 7,000 through diseases, and later on about 6,000 remained in the USA after the war so that only about one half finally returned home. One Hessian soldier who decided to stay wrote home (translated): "-------Staten Island is a hilly country with fine forests, which are a sort of pine, the odor of which one often smells two hours out at sea; but it is really but little settled. The soil is very fertile. Peaches, chestnuts, nuts, apples, pears, and grapevines grow in wild confusion, with roses and blackberry bushes. -----The climate and type of soil are surely the finest, healthiest, and most agreeable in the world; and one or more individuals could prepare a treasure for their posterity. -----One thing more. You know the Huguenot wars in France; what Religion was there, Liberty is here."

These troops were mostly led by German commanders of higher or lower ranks. One was General von Heister. He was a born Hessian and a veteran of many European wars. During these battles, he was severely wounded which left one leg crippled. He was the first Commander of the Hessian troops in America and commanded them in their first battles. Because of a disagreement with his English commander, he was dismissed and returned to Kassel where he soon died thereafter. His replacement was Wilhelm von Knyphausen, also a born Hessian, who had served in many wars in Europe where he finally reached the rank of lieutenant general before he was shipped to England. Under his command, he achieved a number of victories. He was admired by his men because - as it has been reported –he exposed himself to as much fire as a common soldier. He is perhaps also known for stopping the blundering of his soldiers which had been encouraged by von Heister. One Hessian soldier wrote home: "--- but seldom or never did I find a house with the inhabitants in it where war and the wantonness of the English had not ruined everything". Interestingly, he also devised a plot to kidnap George Washington. The plot failed due to a sudden weather change bringing snow and ice. Due to one blind eye and increasing frailty, he finally retired in 1782 with an annual pension of 300 pounds sterling. He returned to Kassel, where he died from the complications of a cataract operation. This was not unusual at this time, since the operation involved sticking a needle into the eye and pressing the lens down. Since neither the lancet nor the hands of the operator were clean, infections would often be fatal.

After the war. After the war, American loyalists were treated badly. They were harassed and physically assaulted. They were driven from their properties or hanged from trees. Many Tories tried to escape to Canada and this number has been estimated to have been close to 100,000. Among them must have been quite a number of German loyalists but no official record exists of their number (65-76).

In summary, many newly immigrated Germans and German-Americans fought in this war but mostly on the side of the Colonists. Here, they contributed significantly to victory, independence and the continuation of the United States of America. Baron von Steuben has to be mentioned foremost who drilled colonists into solid soldiers which eventually won the war. A number of German colonists while hoping for independence refused to fight in the Colonial Army due to their religious beliefs. However, they suffered great personal and economic headships for their actions. A few American colonists and German immigrants also fought on the British side but most Germans fighting for the Crown were the auxiliary" Hessians". Many of these soldiers died here. A fair number of these soldiers decided to stay in America for good after the war. The loyalists were badly treated after the war and many fled to Canada among them most likely was a fair number of German-Americans.

THE 1900TH CENTURY AND CIVIL WAR

The nineteenth century saw a large influx of Germans into the United States estimated to be six to eight million or more. Part of this influx was the failed German revolution and an ever impoverished lower class in Germany.

German revolution. At this time, Germany was still divided into a number of larger and smaller principalities. Each of them was ruled with absolute power by a particular sovereign. Some principalities had even a parliament which, however, possessed no or little power. While some of these sovereigns elected a "Kaiser" (Emperor), the power rested with the individual sovereigns. Thus, the German bourgeois and working class wanted to have more say in the political affairs of a state and they also wanted to have a more united Germany.

After some of these democratic ideas became popular, they were well received by the lower and middle classes. This resulted in demonstrations which led to confrontations between residents and soldiers in various cities as well as the deaths of some civilians. Thus, a central parliament was formed in Frankfurt to discuss these matters and to formulate a new, more democratic German Constitution. Unfortunately, members of the Parliament turned out to be very much divided in their opinions and did not accomplish very much.

Unrest in the cities grew but was quickly suppressed. A few battles between the revolutionaries and the mercenaries of the sovereigns were won by the latter. Again, mercenaries proofed to be the better soldiers. Finally, the parliament in Frankfurt was dissolved and the sovereigns restored their former power. They continued to rule as before or established their own parliaments which, however, again lacked any serious decision making. The promising efforts to achieve a more democratic influence into politics had failed and the idea of a more unified Germany had vanished as well. Revolutionaries who had dared to defy royal authorities were forced to pay the penalty of harassment, exile, economic ruin, imprisonment or even death. Many of the political concessions made earlier, under the pressure of popular turmoil, were now restricted or abrogated (77-79)

In addition to the failed revolution and perhaps fueled by it, Germany started to industrialize. While industrialization generally benefits the population in the long run, it usually starts with a rising income inequality and dismal living conditions of the urban working class. And indeed at this time, the working class suffered from low wages, long working hours, unemployment, sickness and bad housing conditions. Their living conditions were truly miserable (79).

German immigration. All of these factors played a major role in the influx of German immigrants into the United States. Ex-revolutionaries had to flee from persecution or were seeking the country of their "dreams" – a well functioning democracy. Poorer individuals came with the hope to find better job opportunities in the big cities or the wide open lands of America.

First among them was a small group of "Rappists". These people were followers of John George Rapp, born in Iptingen, Wuerttenberg. They believed that Christ would return during their life time and later started to practice celibacy. Persecuted in Germany, they came to America around 1804, established the Harmony Society and founded the community Harmony in Pennsylvania. Over time, this group was economically very successful and became the wealthiest of all such religious groups. The city of Harmony in Pennsylvania still exists today (80).

The most well know immigrant was perhaps John Jacob Astor. He was born in Waldorf, Baden-Wuerttenberg, and immigrated to the States in 1784 with $ 25 to his name. However, he was quite a business man. With many shrewd and successful real estate dealings, in particular with the Indians, and the founding of the American Fur Company became the richest man in America at this time with a wealth estimated to be 20 million Dollars (400 million of today's money) at his death. However, he was also a philanthropist and bequeathed $400,000 for the founding of a Public Library in New York. The "Astor Library" later was consolidated with others as the New York Public Library in 1895 (82).

Another interesting fact is that a group of Nobilities formed the "Adelsverein" (Nobility Society) in Germany and they later tried to establish an independent Monarchy in Texas. They claimed this to become "the new Fatherland on the other side of the ocean". Thus, Prince Carl of Solms-Braunfels sailed to America in 1844 with three ships and 150 families to establish this colony. They named it New Braunfels and later on gave it the name of "Kingdom of Adelsverein". The colony was quite successful and prospered. Early on they even established a news paper "Neu Braunfelser Zeitung (New Braunfels newspaper) which still exists as the New Braunfels-Harald Zeitung. After solidly establishing the Kingdom, he returned to Germany where he died. The Adelsverein with American soldiers then attacked successfully Mexico and gained a large amount of land. America recognized the "Kingdom of Adelsverein" even as an independent Nation. In 1849, slavery was made illegal and the kingdom joined the Union during the Civil war. It was promised that it will be treated as part of the homeland, not as a colony. At the end of the century, the Kingdom of Adelsverein slowly disintegrated with some people staying in Texas, some moving to other parts of the country and some returning to Germany. Today, there are about 30,000 individuals who claim to be descendants of the Adelsverein. Nevertheless, of interest is that at one time in American history there existed a Kingdom on "American" soil for a number of years (83).

Among the many other immigrants was Margaretha Meyer Schurz who was born in Hamburg to a liberal Jewish family and who established the first "Kindergarten" (Children's garden) with 5 children in Watertown, Wisconsin. Today, the name has persisted and there are now kindergartens all over the United States (84).

Another German-born American was Mathilde Franziska Anneke, born as a Giesler but later adopting her husband's name of Anneke. She was an early advocate of women's political and social rights. She was born in Lerchenhausen, Westphalia; and later on fought along her husband in the German revolution. After its failure, she had to flee to America in about 1850.In Milwaukee; she began publishing a militant monthly newsletter about women's rights, the "Deutsche Frauenzeitung" (German Women's Newspaper) and addressed the women's rights convention in New York City. She fought for female education and opened a progressive girls' school. Later on, she founded a women's suffrage association in Wisconsin. Her work contributed significantly to the later success of women's liberation (85).

The last is a man whose achievements can still be seen in New York – The Brooklyn Bridge. This man was John Augustus Roebling. He was born in Muehlhausen, Thuringia and later studied engineering and started to develop an interest in suspension bridges. In 1831, Roebling left Prussia because engineers had great difficulty in obtaining jobs in his home country. In America, he improved the design of various suspension bridges and built a number of smaller bridges. But his main achievement is the Brooklyn Bridge which he conceived and which still stands proudly today with its magnificent structure. The construction of the Brooklyn Bridge began in 1869. During surveying the Brooklyn Bridge, he sustained an injury that resulted in his death. Before he died, he put his son Washington in charge of the project. Washington was also injured on the job site and had to supervise the work from his apartment. His wife Emily became the go-between between Washington and the construction crews. Emily Roebling was the first woman field engineer and became an expert during its construction. She was also the first person to cross the bridge after opening ceremonies. The whole project took 11 years (86).

Among the many immigrants were also a few entrepreneurs who founded businesses and companies of their interest and skills. Many of these were short lived or were quickly bought by other companies. But a few withstood the test of time, grew into large corporations and are still with us today.

Let us start with the German beer brewers who arrived in the nineteenth century. All these beer brewers knew that Germans love beer and in particular German beer which was a bit different from the American brewed one. So they started their own breweries wherever there was a large German population.

In 1829, the German beer brewer David Gottlieb Jüngling from Aldingen, Wuerttenberg, immigrated to the United States and opened a brewery called "Eagle Brewery" in Pottsville, near Philadelphia. He anglicized his name from Jüngling meaning in German "young man"to the English name: Yuengling. When his son joined the father, the "Eagle Brewery" became the "D. G. Yuengling and Son Brewery" in 1873.Although the company's name changed, the bald eagle remained the company's emblem. It is believed to be the oldest German beer brewery and is still going strong. Today, Yuengling produces about 3 million barrels of beer.

The next is Friedrich Eberhard Johannes Mueller, born in Riedlingen, Wuerttemberg, who came to this country in 1824 where he changed his name into Frederick Miller. In Germany, he had learned how to brew beer and had saved some money. So when he entered the States, he not only had $ 8000 in gold but also carried a special kind of beer yeast with him. He settled in Milwaukee and bought a small beer brewing company and named it "Miller Brewery". He quickly expanded the company but fell on hard times during prohibition which the company survived by selling cereal beverages, soft drinks, and malt-related products. The company started with about 25 employees and produced about 300 barrels of beer at this time. Now it has about 10 000 employees and brews about 40 million barrels.

Jacob Best, born in Mettenheim, Hessen, moved to America in 1844. Here, he founded with his 4 sons "The Jacob Best and Sons Brewery" in Milwaukee. Twenty years later, Phillip's son-in-law Frederick Pabst joined the company. Frederick was born in Nikolausrieth, Prussia and came to this country at the age of 20. He first worked at various ships and finally became captain of his own ship. After the ship was badly damaged, he joined the Best brewery. He proved to be a very inventive and successful brewer and soon the company became known as the "The Pabst Brewing Company". The *Milwaukee Sentinel* wrote in the summer of 1892: "If the question was put anywhere in the world to-day, "Which is the largest lager beer brewery?" a school boy would answer, so well is the name known, "The Pabst Brewing Company". If curiosity should occasion a second question, "By whose ability has this brewery reached such phenomenal sales?" the reply would be "Frederick Pabst". Today, this company sells about 5 million barrels of beer as one of the largest American beer brewing companies.

And then there was the founding of the Anheuser-Busch brewery. Eberhard Anheuser was born in Bad Kreuznach, Rhineland –Palatinate, and left Germany in 1843. He was trained as a soap manufacturer but became part owner of a Bavarian Brewery in St. Louis. On the other hand, Adolphus Busch was born in Castel near Mainz, and made his way to St. Louis in 1857. Adolphus had some brewing experience by selling brewing equipment. By chance, he met the daughter of Anheuser, married her and joined his father-in-law to found the "Anheuser-Busch Brewery". There flagship beer was "Budweiser – a name chosen because it could easily be pronounced by German and English speaking consumers at that time. Busch proofed to be very inventive and became the first American brewer to use pasteurization so that beer could be stored and shipped long distances. In 1880, he introduced artificial refrigeration into beer transports. These technological innovations allowed the company to grow rapidly. Today, they produce about 35 million barrels of beer.

In 1848, Georg August Krug born in Miltenberg, Bavaria, came to the USA to established a restaurant in Kilbourntown (now central Milwaukee). Soon after, he added a small brewery and produced 150 barrels of beer the first year. As the brewery slowly grew, he built the first underground brewer's vault by digging and tunneling into a nearby hill. This provided the consistent cool environment which is essential to brewing and storing beer. As the company grew, more help was hired among them a Joseph Schlitz. Joseph was born in Mainz and entered the States about 1845. After Krug's death, he married his widow and the company became the "Schlitz "company with its famous slogan:"If you are out of Schlitz- you are out of beer". It became one of the largest breweries around 1900 until it was acquired by the Pabst Company.

In 1867, Adolph Hermann Joseph Kuhrs came to America. He was born in Prussia and learned there how to properly brew beer. He then ventured as a penniless stowaway to America. After working at various jobs in Chicago, he had saved enough money to found with a friend a brewery. Since the English did pronounce his name Kuhrs like "coors" he changed his name to Coors and also dropped the last n in Hermann. After paying out his friend, the brewery became the "Coors Brewing Company". The company became very successful and is now one of the largest beer brewing companies employing about 10 000 employees. However, there are some tragic events connected to this family. Adolph Coors died from a fall from his hotel window while vacationing in Virginia and it was never established if this was a suicide or homicide. Later on, the grandson of the Coors founder and then chairman of the brewery was kidnapped in the 1960s and held for ransom before being shot to death (87-90, 145,148).

In addition to the beer makers, the German wine makers did not miss their calling and also came to America at this time. America was full of native grape vines when the very first settlers arrived (and they called it "Vinland"). However, the grapes produced a wine which was not to the taste of the European settlers. Early settlers in Pennsylvania already tried to produce wine but it did not taste well and did not last. Wineries in other states also were founded and they also produced wine for only short periods of time. Thus, vines from France, Italy, Spain, Mexico and Germany were gradually introduced and were interbred with American vines to make more pest resistant plants. But vineries had a rough beginning until the 1830. After this time wine caught the taste of the American people. Quickly, French, Mexican and Italian entrepreneurs founded wineries in California and the West coast. Of course, German wine makers arrived and participated in the fledgling wine making industry.

Charles Krug, born in Trentleburg, Prussia, came to America in 1847 and moved to San Francisco in 1853. He was actually a barber but obtained his knowledge of wine making by working at various wineries in California until he founded the "Krug Vinery" in 1861. This winery is by now the oldest winery in the NAPA valley. It did very well and already produced 800 000 gallons of wine just before prohibition. In 1943, the winery was bought by the Mondavis. Today, the"Mondavi Winery" is perhaps the largest wine producer with about 75 million cases sold per year.

Emil Dresel, son of a famous champagne producer in Weisenheim, Palatine. came to California in 1857 in search of his fortune. With him, however, he brought some vine cuttings from his family's vineyard. These were most likely the first Riesling and Sylvaner varieties introduced into the United States. He and Joseph Gundlach, a born Bavarian, bought land and basically founded a winery, called "Rheinfarm" (Rhine Farm).. They were later joined in 1868 by Charles Bundschu, originally from Mannheim, as well as Emil's brother Julius. It was Julius who saved the winery in 1878 from a devastating plague. At this time, Phylloxera, a tiny insect, had threatened to wipe out the entire grape vine stock in America. Thus, Julius became the first grower in the state to plant vineyards with disease resistant vines. The grafting system he used revived the industry and it is still used until today. Today, there are no Dresels or Grundlachs anymore, but the principals of "Rhinefarm" are the Bundschus.

Perhaps the best known of all the early German immigrants to the Wine Country were the Beringer brothers, Frederick and Jacob, from Mainz. In 1875, they bought 215 acres in St. Helena and started the " Beringer Brothers Winery". To make ends meet, one brother worked temporarily as a cellar superintendent at the nearby Krug Winery. The winery proved to be a success and even during prohibition it continued to produce wine – but this time smartly for religious reasons and was sold as sacramental wine to churches.

Another German involved with wine albeit not making but studying it was Eugene W. Hilgard. His lawyer father had left Germany with his family for political reasons. Eugene was then raised in the States. Later he went to Germany to study agriculture at the Heidelberg University. After his return in 1853, he became the first professor of agriculture at the University of California in Berkeley. He introduced scientific methodologies in viticulture and enology to produce high-quality wine from California-grown grapes. Some of these scientific methods and principles are still being used

Germans also founded wineries in other States. For instance, Friedrich Muench, a Lutheran minister from Niedergemuenden, Hesse, founded a winery in Missouri in 1859. This winery is still in existence today. Muench once wrote:" With the growth of the grape, every nation elevates itself to a higher degree of civilization". Similarly, wine making was tried in other states as well but it was less successful until much later (91-98). . .

Just as important is the fact that German butchers also arrived in America. They knew that Germans like sausages and pork and that there was a need since Americans did not make sausages and preferred beef. The earliest slaughter houses were established in Cincinnati which was referred to as "Porkopolis". As early as 1833, these slaughter houses processed already more than 85,000 pigs a year. Tokens from this time include the name of a butcher by the name of Jacob Knauber of whom little is known. More is known about a German immigrant who founded a meat packing company. His name is Ferdinand Sulzberger, born in Obergrombach, Baden, and immigrated to America in 1863. He first worked as clerk in

New York until he entered a small slaughtering business that had been established some ten years before by a Joseph Schwarzschild, forming the partnership of Schwarzschild and Sulzberger. Again, Schwarzschild's name tells us that he must have been of German origin. However, the general literature search did not reveal anything about him. The company did well but after 1900 was acquired by various other companies and the name was lost.

Later on, Chicago became the center of the meat packing industry when it opened the Union Stock Yard in 1865. At its peak, more than 18 million livestock were slaughtered annually and, amazingly, the grim mechanization of death of the slaughter houses attracted thousands upon thousands of tourists—including European royalties. It also led to the book "The Jungle" written in 1906. The book describes the harsh conditions and exploited lives of workers including German immigrants in Chicago and other cities. Its primary purpose was to draw attention to the horrible working conditions and the inhuman slaughter or animals. While it might have eased some of them, the government was more concerned with the related health issues. This led to some health related reforms including the Meat Inspection Act to make the consumption of meat safer. At its peak time, the work force consisted of 30% of German immigrants.

Another butchers was Moritz Beisinger who was born in Hechingen, Wuertenberg into a cattle raising family. After the revolution, the family's property was confiscated and young Moritz was sent to America. Here, he changed his name to Nelson Morris and started to trade cattle which lead him later to move to Chicago. There he bought a slaughter house and butcher shop and founded "Morris and Company". Selling meat to the union army made the company grow quickly and within the next 20 years it was a successful meat packing companies with annual sales of then $ 100 million. The company later went through mergers, dissolutions and acquisitions but is still in existence as "Morris Meat Packing".

Oscar Ferdinand Mayer, another butcher, was born in Koesingen, Wuerttemberg, In 1873, he immigrated to America at the age of 14 for unknown reasons and worked in a meat packing company in Chicago. Here, he planned to open up a butcher and sausage company. While he worked at various jobs to save money, he asked his brother Gottfried in Germany to learn how to make good sausages. A few years later, at the age of 24 he and his brother, who also had immigrated to America, opened a butcher and sausage making shop. They sold good old German "Blutwurst" (blood sausage), " Leberwurst" (liver sausage or liverwurst), Frankfurter and Bratwurst and not to forget "Speck" (bacon). After some initial troubles, the company became very successful and employed 9000 workers at the time of his death in 1955. It even had its own song: "I wish I were an Oscar Mayer Weiner -that is what I truly wish to be- cause if I were an Oscar Mayer Weiner-everyone would be in love – oh, everyone would be in love- everyone would be in love with me". And not to forget is its Weiner automobile which consisted of a low chassis carrying a large Weiner.

These early German immigrants also contributed to some new meat dishes. In the early stages, slaughter houses would throw ribs into the river. Early German immigrants are believed to have collected these as a cheap meat source and did make them into spare ribs. One Philadelphian, boarding in Cincinnati, wrote home "What a splendid table my landlady, Mrs. G. keeps. She gives us spare ribs for breakfast four or five times a week. The fact is she can get a basket filled at any pork house in the city by sending for them and not paying a cent". Here in Cincinnati, "goetta" was also developed by unknown German immigrants most likely from northwestern regions of Oldenburg, Hannover, and Westphalia.

Goetta is primarily composed of ground meat, either pork or pork and beef, oats and spices. It is still a favorable dish in and around Cincinnati.

Albeit not an immigrant per se, Henry John Heinz cannot be forgotten. His parents were born in Germany but immigrated to America. They made their way to Pittsburgh, where Henry was born in 1844. When Henry turned 10, the parents granted him 3,000 square meters of land, and at the age of 12, he was the owner of 12,000 squares meters of land. Gardens and vegetables became his obsession. Shortly, thereafter, he made horseradish and sold it in glass-containers to show that his product was pure (since deceit was rampant at this time). He was also quite a shrewd businessman by sending his first product sample under a false name to the customer and only if it proved successful, would he put his real name on it. Unfortunately, due to circumstances beyond his control, the business went bankrupt. After a while, with all the savings of his mother, he started to make and sell tomato sauce which was originally based on a recipe from his mother. This was the beginning of the "Heinz Company". His early product was named "catsup" later changed to "ketchup. The business was a great success and today the company employs more than 30 000 workers and has revenues of more than 12 billion dollars. On a personal note, while vacationing in Germany, World War I broke out and he was placed under house arrest and could have detained for an uncertain time. However, he managed to escape to Holland and from there back home (98-103).

Another company which started in America and became a successful company was "The Piano Manufacturing Company of Steinway and sons". The carpenter and music instrument maker Heinrich Engelhardt Steinweg was born in Wolfshagen near Braunschweig and immigrated with his sons to this country in 1849. Here, he changed his name to Henry E Steinway and founded in

1853 the Steinway Company in New York. In 1880, some years after Steinway's death, his sons returned to Germany and established also a production site in Hamburg to meet rising demands in Europe. Today, Steinway & Sons is one of the leading piano manufacturers in the world producing pianos of the highest quality. Every musician and music lover knows the word "Steinway".

At last, a household word – Levis jeans. Loeb Strauss was born in Buttenheim, Bavaria. At age 18, Strauss traveled with his mother and two sisters to the United States to join the brothers Jonas and Louis, who had begun a wholesale dry goods business in New York City called "J. Strauss Brother & Co". He changed his name to Levi Strauss. He and Jacob Davis tried to make working pants stronger by using heavier material and adding metal rivets in places where there was much strain on the pants. They received a U.S. patent for an "Improvement in Fastening Pocket-Openings." The pants became an instant success. They advertised the new pants with the "Horse Trademark". Even two horses could not pull apart a pair of Levi's® waist pants. Using blue denim, these pants became known later as Jeans. Levi Strauss & Co. introduced the first blue jeans for women in 1934. By the 1960s, the popularity of jeans revolutionized the entire business attire when young professionals adopted jeans as their pants of choice and lead the change in making casual wear an appropriate attire for the workplace. Today, this company is a billion dollar company (99-103,146-148).

Civil war. The Civil war was another factor which made some Germans immigrate and where they then fought on either side. The causes of the war were increasing differences between North and South. The South wanted retention and expansion of slavery while the North wanted to abolish slavery. The North was industrialized while the South was agricultural. The last major problem was the belief in strong states rights by the South while the North favored a more central government. Because of the election of Abraham Lincoln, South Carolina ceded from the Union in 1860 which was, quickly followed by Mississippi, Florida, Alabama, Georgia, Louisiana and Texas. Together they formed the Confederate States of America in 1861 with Jefferson Davis becoming its President. Fighting started in 1861 with the confederates firing on Fort Sumter (and some businesses immediately started to take advantage of the situation – see advertisement) .The Confederates were commanded by General Lee while the Union supreme commanders changed with General Grant being the last.

The first battle at Bull Run was quickly followed by a series of minor and major battles most of them being fought on southern soil. In the beginning, the South was successful which changed during the war and at the end the North won the war. This was not unexpected because the North outnumbered the South 4 to 1 in man power and had the backing of its industrial machinery. The Civil War was America's bloodiest conflict. The total number of casualties is estimated to be about 600,000 to 700,000 deaths with, for instance. the battle at Gettysburg alone contributing about 10.000 fatalities and about 30.000 wounded (104-106).

Businesses quickly saw sales opportunities and they advertised in German and in English (English version):

WAR TIMES AND WAR PRICES
RETAIL, WITHOUT PROFIT

Eight Dollars in Money will buy you a coat and pants
Nine Dollars in Money will buy you a fine coat and vest
Et cetera

German Participation in the war. At this time, as mentioned above, a large number of Germans had immigrated to this country as result of the failed revolution of 1848. They were also called the "forty-eighters". And when the war started Germans and American Germans were asked to enlist with posters reading like:

ACHTUNG DEUTSCHE
1. Deutsche Kentucky Regiment
Unterzeichnete sind beauftragt fuer das
erste deutsche Regiment, welches
hier in Louisville organisiert wird, Soldaten anzuwerben.
Dollar 13 werden im Voraus bezahlt und
die Familien der Freiwilligen
werden von der Stadt fuer den Kriegsdienst unterhalten.

Kansig
Marter

(Translation: Attention Germans- 1.Kentucky regiment. – The undersigned are ordered for the first German regiment, which is here organized in Louisville, to enlist soldiers - 13 dollars are paid in advance and the families of the volunteers will be supported by the town during the war time service – Kansig and Marter)

Again, German immigrants and German Americans joined one of the two sides and again confronted each other in battle. It has been estimated that about 220 000 German born Americans and German immigrants fought in this war with the majority being in the Union Army. While most newly arrived Germans fought in ethnically mixed regiments, some of them fought in purely German regiments commanded by German officers. Since language was still a problem with many of the immigrants but also with some of the German Americans, German regiments were preferred because commands would be easier understood and communication among the soldiers was easier. This lack of the command of the English language is shown in that many advertisements to enlist were written in plain German.

Many of the German immigrants who had previous military or war experience in Europe were particularly welcomed. And there were quite a few. At this time in Europe, there were always military conflicts in one or the other corner and many men had to make a living by joining the state's army, selling themselves as mercenaries or were rented out by their sovereign to fight for other sovereigns. Thus, many were battle hardened veterans who came voluntarily to America to serve as soldiers where they would get paid and after the war, if they survived, had a better chance to make a more decent living than in their home country,

At this time, soldiers and officers were accompanied by drummer boys aged about 14. Drummer boys would set the marching pace and sometimes provided cadence for the firing of guns and cannons. One of the youngest and perhaps most famous was John Joseph Klem. He was born to German immigrant parents, Roman and Magdalene Klem, in 1851 in Newark, Ohio. Later on, the family changed their name to Clem. John tried to enlist in the Union Army at the age of ten, but his request was refused. Due to his never ending requests, he finally was accepted two years later to follow the army as a mascot and unofficial drummer boy. At one of the battles, history has it that a Confederate force surrounded his troop at Chickamauga. A Confederate colonel spotted Clem and shouted to drop his weapon. Rather than surrender, Clem shot the colonel and successfully made his way back to Union lines. For his actions, Clem was promoted to sergeant, the youngest soldier ever to become a noncommissioned officer in the U.S. Army. Thereafter, he became known as the "Drummer Boy of Chickamauga". After the war, he continued his army career and died as a major general.

And one should not forget the women. Any army at these times was usually accompanied by a large number of women who were either the wives of soldiers or officers or were ladies" of ill repute". Prostitution was legal or it was not enforced. Thus, some women took advantage of this opportunity to make some money. Since General Hooker of the Union Army allowed prostitutes to follow his army, these women were claimed to have been called "Hookers". However, another version of the origin of the word hooker said that the slang name came from an area in New York called Hook known for its many brothels and wide spread prostitution. However, little is known about these women and only more recently discovered was the fact that a small number actually fought in the war. This could easily have been done by using a male fake name and medical examinations for enlistment were short or were not done at all. They did so for many different reasons. Often, the main reason was not to be separated from their husbands. However, patriotism, the desire for adventure and the opportunity to improve their legal, economic, and social status did also play a role. Because of their male disguise and a faked male name, they could now purchase land, take advantage of more abundant and better paying jobs and even vote. And it was only after these women were wounded or killed that their true identity became known. Among these women, there was also a German woman known only by her male alias, "Charles Junghaus" . Little is known about her except she did fight in several battles. She was described in a letter as being:" tan, dirty, freckled but courageous" (107-108).

Germans fighting with the Union Army. Many newly arrived Germans joined the Union army quickly since they were against slavery which was unknown in Germany. Many also had experienced rural "serfdom" in their home country where they had little rights and were at the mercy of the land owner. One Immigrant wrote home (translated)" "I've seen it often enough how the poor slaves are sold away from their wives and children and beaten with a whip until their skin hangs in tatters." Germans also wanted to preserve the unity of the States which they had not achieved in their homeland. They also had not forgotten that the aristocracy had helped to squash the German revolution and they viewed the South as being ruled by the aristocracy. One of the enlistment slogans for enlistment was:' "protect our new republican homeland against the aristocracy of the South". But last but not least, many German immigrants were grateful to America for accepting them and they were willing to fight for this affection. Sergeant Albert Krause wrote home (translated): ""The United States has taken me in, I have earned a living here. Why shouldn't I defend them…with my flesh and blood?" An immigrant's mother proclaimed at an antislavery convention in New York :" I am from Germany where my brothers all fought against the Government and tried to make us free, but were unsuccessful ---We foreigners know the preciousness of that great, noble gift a great deal better than you, because you never were in slavery, but we were born in it".

However, some were enlisted without knowing what actually had happened. William Albrecht after his arrival in America wrote to his family in Germany (translated):" We landed in Castle Garden [New York]---as soon as you set foot in the country, the recruiters came at you from all sides. Since I didn't know anything about American recruiting tricks, I did the same thing as others…I signed up." Albrecht soon regretted his "mistake" of enlisting in an "American" unit, deserted and joined a German-speaking artillery unit instead.

There were two German immigrants who helped the Union army to enlist enough soldiers. One was Franz Sigel. He was born in Sinsheim, Wuertenberg, and had participated in the revolution. After the revolution was crushed, he feared for his life and immigrated to America in 1852. He started out in New York and formed the

German-American Institute with his father-in-law. He taught at various schools as well as the German Turner Society (Deutsche Athletic Society). Interestingly, when Abraham Lincoln won the election of 1860, the Turners (athletes) provided his bodyguard at the inauguration. In New York his enlistment cry was:"I goes to fight mit Sigel" (I will fight with Siegel). As war broke out, he joined the Union Army and formed 5 German speaking regiments and commanded them in various battles. The other German Immigrant was Thomas Nast, born in Landau, Baden, whose parents immigrated to America when he was 6. He later studied art at the National Academy of Design and at the age of 15 became a draftsman for Frank Leslie's Illustrated Newspaper and at 18 for Harper's Weekly. With the outbreak of the American Civil War, Nast vigorously supported the cause of the Union and opposed slavery from his drawing board at Harper's Weekly. He also fought city corruption and called for a just treatment of the South after the war. Pres. Abraham Lincoln called him "our best recruiting sergeant"

Another Immigrant was Carl Christian Schurz, born near Cologne, who as an ex revolutionary had to flee Germany after the failed revolution. He moved to Wisconsin in 1852 and became a prominent member of the newly formed Republican Party. He campaigned among German speaking citizens to vote for Abraham Lincoln and these votes in Wisconsin helped Lincoln to become president. At the beginning of the war, he joined as Brigadier General and fought in many battles. After the war, he founded a newspaper and became briefly Secretary of the interior. For his service, the city of new York named one of its parks after him – "The Schurz Park" on the East River. The park surrounds the "Gracie Mansion" – the mansion of the New York mayor.

Similarly, Alexander Schimmelfennig was born in Bromberg, Prussia as Alexander Schimmelpfennig. He first joined the Prussian army but later became acquainted with some of the more radical German political groups and was an active participant in the 1848 revolution. He had to flee and was sentenced to death in absentia. In 1854, Schimmelpfennig immigrated to the United States and gained employment with the War Department. He later joined the Union Army and served as brigadier general in many battles. During this time, he contracted tuberculosis and died at the end of the war.

Overall, there have been 13 German Generals and 200 officers in high positions plus all the unknown soldiers who fought bravely for the Union. Their contribution was so significant that Robert E. Lee allegedly remarked" Take the Germans out of the Union Army and we could whip the Yankees easily". The quote, likely apocryphal, captures their important contribution. What, however, has been actually recorded by a Union officer is:""Let me return to the German soldiers, and state another fact, i.e., that the German soldier is generally far more faithful, conscientious and zealous than the native-born American. This is part of the German nature, which is our reason to be proud of our nation. One more thing: The German soldier is obedient and loyal to duty without regard to reward or punishment. The American generally considers only reward, or — The Guard-House. This is caused by the national education on either side, in the broadest sense of the word". And later on Bell Irwin Wily concludes in his excellent study entitled: The Life of Billy Yank: "On the whole the contribution of this nationality [German] to the union cause was tremendous…. Their neatness, precision and respect for authority were of infinite aid in molding a mob of individuals into an organized fighting force. What the Teutons lacked in quickness and glamour was more than offset by their patience and steadiness, not to mention the idealistic devotion of many of them to the cause of the Union" (109-114).

Germans fighting with the Confederate army. Less is known about Germans fighting in the Confederate Army. But History always favors the winner and the South was the loser. Nevertheless, German Americans and newly immigrated Germans also fought on the side of the Confederate soldiers. Many of these German Americans were descendents from Pennsylvania Dutch settlers who had moved over the years to South Carolina. Many had enlisted because they feared a Union victory would place white people on equal footing with black people or due to loyalties to the state they lived on.

While the Union Army had a number of generals, the highest ranking Germans in the Confederate Army were most likely Colonel Adolphus Heiman and Colonel Augustus Buchel. The first was born in Potsdam, Prussia and had immigrated to the United States in 1834. He spent time in New York before moving to Nashville in1837. Here, as an architect designed many buildings as well as the first bridge over the Cumberland River in Tennessee. The second was born a Buechel in Guntersblum, Hesse, but dropping the umlaut became Buchel. Buchel is said to have gone to Texas in 1845 because he killed a man in a duel in Germany and had to flee. He fought brilliantly in many battles until he was mortally wounded. The best known of the German officers was Johan August Heinrich Heros von Borke known as the "Giant in Gray" due to his height of over 6 feet and his weight of 200 pounds. He was born in Berlin and actually sailed to America as an adventurer in order to join the Confederates in 1862. He became a very close friend of General J.E.B Stuart who achieved fame as a brilliant cavalry commander (115,116).

In summary, The nineteenth century saw the biggest influx of Germans into America estimated to have been 8 million. The reasons were the failed German revolution of 1848 and the poor state of the economy with the lower classes getting more and more impoverished. These immigrants made significant contributions. Some founded long lasting companies in beer brewing, wine making and meat processing as well other industries. Some left their mark in engineering or in promoting women's liberation. Many fought bravely in the Civil war and it is believed that these Germans in the Union Army helped significantly to win the war and to preserve The United States of America as we know it today.

THE 20TH CENTURY UP
TO WORLD WAR I

German immigration. From 1900 until 1920, immigrants still arrived but their numbers had decreased markedly. It almost stopped completely during World War I and after the war was then limited by newly formed laws (see Ellis Island) to about 25,000 persons per year for the years 1924 and 1929.

German Russian immigration. Around 1900, there was a massive influx of German speaking immigrants to America but these immigrants did not come from Germany but from Russia. According to the American Historical Society of Germans From Russia, these Germans had first immigrated to Russia and its territories like Poland and Ukraine. The reasons for their migration to these areas were more or less the same as the reasons why Germans came to America. People tried to escape religious persecution, the unending feuds and wars among the various German principalities, the shackles of serfdom and utter poverty.

In 1763, Czarina Catherine II, a former German princess, needing skilled craftsmen and farmers offered any German immigrant a wonderful proposal including unqualified religious freedom, freedom from taxation and licenses for 30 years, a guarantee of self-rule within the colonies, no military service for all settlers and their descendents and free transport to areas of settlement. Thus, many Germans accepted this offer since the distance and cost for their move were so much more favorable as those to America. Soon, more than 100,000 Germans mostly from Hesse and the Rhineland migrated to Russia. Some settled near the Volga River (they named it "Wiesenseite" or Meadow Site) while others went to the Black Sea and some near Kiew. Again, most faced some major problems at arrival mostly being the winter and the lands were in half-savaged areas. But nevertheless, they received 80 acres, a wagon, plow, horses and tools. Their first homes were primitive sod houses.

Like in America, the lived in close knit colonies, cultivated their German heritage and spoke mostly German. Like American settlers who were often harassed and attacked by Indians, so were these settlers by nomadic tribes who preyed on these hapless victims. Unfamiliar with the climate in their new homeland, farming was often conducted wrongly leading to massive crop failures. Up to one fifths of the settlers died within the first years or was sold into slavery. But by 1800, the young colonies began to blossom and became the agricultural pacesetters of Russia. Now they were efficient farmers and cattle breeders. Gradually, windmills and steam-driven mills for grain and weaving were built, and dye works came into existence. Economic growth made these communities prosper and the population started to grow.

Then unease settled in. The Czar Alexander II repealed all privileges in1871with the slogan: "One Czar, one religion, one language!" Since passage to America has become easier, many of these German Russians decided to leave Russia and began to immigrate to America. The first group came to America in 1872 and settled in the Dakotas. The next group came in 1873 and settled in Nebraska. The heaviest influx was during the years after the Russian famine in 1890 to the Revolution in 1917. By 1920, it has been estimated that nearly 300,000 Germans Russians had come to America. Today, about 1 million Americans claim ethnic German Russian descent.

Early immigration helped in that the American Railroads Companies needing workers had sent emissaries to Russia to actively persuade these German Russians to come to America and work on the railroads and to offer them land for farming. Here, they helped to build the early railroads and established a new farming system in these areas. It was a Bernhard Warkentin who introduced a harder wheat species into Kansas successfully replacing the commonly used softer and more vulnerable wheat variety. They founded many future cities named Odessa and Moscow. Among other immigrants or their descendants were Irving Berlin born as Israel Beilin, Georg Gershwin born Jacob Bruskin Gershowitz, the biologist Theodosius Dozhansky, Michael Bloomberg, Bernie Sanders and many more. However, what most cherished was that they found freedom. In contrast, the ones who remained in Russia soon suffered losses of their homes, starvation, deportation to Siberia and severe persecution during the Bolshevik revolution and World War II (117).

Ellis Island. This Island became at this time a major entrance point for most immigrants. This island in front of New York was named for the Manhattan merchant Samuel Ellis, who owned it in the 1770s. For a time, it was used as a dumping ground for ballasts from ships and these provided landfill and extended the area of the island considerably. In 1808, the State of New York sold the island to the federal government which used it as a fort and a powder magazine. Finally, in 1892 it became the nation's first major immigration station. Then a major fire destroyed most of the buildings but it was quickly rebuilt in a fire proof manner. In 1924, it was closed after an approximate 12 million immigrants had passed through its gates. For a short time, it served as a detention station for aliens and deportees until 1954. After extensive restorations and renovations, it is now open to the public and it is worthwhile seeing,

When Ellis Island opened, a great change was taking place with U.S. immigration. Up to this point, individual states had been in charge of immigration. But now, the federal government took control of immigration for all states with Ellis Island being the main entry point. This was followed by the immigrant Quota Act of 1921 and the National Origins Act of 1924, which limited the numbers and nationalities of immigrants allowed into the United States.

At this time, immigration would actually start when passengers would enter a ship. A ship's officer would ask for and record first and family names. No identification was required. Thus, some passengers would give a wrong name or could not verify the correct spelling of their names because they could neither write nor read. Then the ship would leave harbor and made its voyage across the ocean.

Before the ship was allowed to enter into New York Harbor, it had to stop at a quarantine checkpoint off the coast of Staten Island. Here, doctors would board the ship and look for dangerous and contagious diseases such as smallpox, yellow fever, plague, cholera and leprosy. Once the ship passed inspection, immigration officers began boarding the ship via rope ladders. Then the ship would proceed and dock in New York Harbor. First- and second-class passengers were quickly interviewed and could leave the ship. Everything was done verbally and no papers were needed except the ship's documents filled out at the beginning of the trip. This process was kept short because these passengers being able to afford the price of the upper classes were not considered to become a burden to the States later on.

All other passengers were given tags so that inspectors could identify these passengers later on. They were then confronted by U.S. customs officers who would quickly check bags for dutiable goods or contraband. The passengers were then put aboard small steamboats and brought to Ellis Island. These boats would carry up to 1,000 passengers.

At Ellis Island, according to Barry Moreno, historian and librarian at the Ellis Island Immigration Museum, the passengers would be ordered to form two separate lines. One line was for women and their children under the age of 15 and the other line for men. Here, they were checked by physicians for eye, skin, heart and other obvious diseases. These physicians quickly established their own identification system by placing a letter with chalk on the cloth of the immigrant. An 'H' indicated heart trouble, 'L' suspected lameness; 'X' suspected feeble-mindedness, and so on. Those individuals with marks were removed from the line and placed in the "doctor's pen" .Here, the doctors could later on conduct further examinations. Only about 10 percent of people were detained for this kind of examination. The majority would move with the line until questioned by an inspector sometimes in the presence of an interpreter. The inspector would verify the passenger manifest by reading the information provided by the ship's list. If everything was OK, he would just make a little check mark by the name. This meant that inspection had been passed successfully and the person was free to go. This could be as short as 3-4 hrs from the time of arrival at the station. No official paperwork was provided to the person. However, if the answers were bad, wrong or suspicious or if secret information had arrived about a person before his or her arrival, they would be detained. A decision would then be reached which could mean weeks or months of detainment.

This process at Ellis Island had to be fast because on some days there were up to 5, 000 immigrants to be processed. Between 1892 and 1954 records show that about 12 million immigrants were processed.

It is often said that during this process names were intentionally and unintentionally been misspelled or changed. This is incorrect because no written records were made. Officials relied only on the records received from the ship and all communications were verbal. Thus, if name changes have occurred, they originated intentionally or unintentionally with the ship's lists.

It must have been quite a frightening experience for most German immigrants to go through the lines at Ellis Island and are being confronted by physicians and inspectors – all in uniform and all speaking a foreign language (118,119).

World War 1. This war had a major impact not only on the immigration of Germans to America but perhaps more so on the lives and fate of German Americans right here in this country. World War I was triggered by the assassination of the Archduke of Austria-Hungary and officially began on July 28, 1914, when Austria-Hungary declared war on Serbia. This seemingly small conflict between these two countries spread rapidly due to various non –aggression treaties among a number of countries. Initially, the countries involved were Germany, Austria-Hungary, Russia, Great Britain, and France. Later on the Ottoman Empire (Turkey) and in 1917 America entered the war. The latter tried to be neutral for a long time but was finally drawn into the war mainly by the German decision to sink neutral merchant ships which entered England waters in order to dock in one of the harbors.. Germans feared that these ships would not only bring food but military equipment and ammunition as well. The breaking point was the sinking of the passenger ship Lusitania with hundreds of American lives being lost before the Coast of England.

While the Lusitania was flying a neutral flag indicating that it would not transport heavy war material illegally to England, there is evidence that the Lusitania actually might have carried large amounts of ammunition. This is indicated that the two German torpedoes which struck the ship should not have caused the recorded large explosions and extensive damage resulting in the ship sinking within about 20 minutes unless the torpedoes hit hidden ammunition. Eye witnesses also stated that they heard a second explosion after the torpedo hit which again indicates an explosion of present ammunition. This sinking killed 1,198 passengers leaving 761 survivors. Among the 128 American passengers killed, was Alfred Gwynne Vanderbilt, a member of the very wealthy Vanderbilt family. America blamed Germany for the loss of American lives and shortly thereafter entered the war in 1917. With the entrance of America, the war turned to favor the English-France-American Alliance and Germany and Austria-Hungary finally had to capitulate. The war ended November 11, 1981 with the Treaty of Versailles which punished Germany with hefty economic reparations, territorial losses, and strict limits on its rights to possess an army.

It has been estimated that the war took the lives of more than 9 million soldiers; 21 million more were wounded and some crippled for life. Civilian casualties caused indirectly by the war numbered close to 10 million. German casualties have been estimated to have been about 7 million killed, wounded, or missing in action (120).

Anti-German-American sentiment. Before World War 1, most immigrants from Germany had assimilated well into the American culture but they still were somewhat distinct from others because of the use of the German language. German was the most used and studied foreign language at this time. It has been estimated that there were more than 500 German news papers around 1900. Germans were quite proud of their native tongue and used it to communicate among each other, taught it in schools, preached it in churches and used it in their clubs and unions. They also favored their special German food, German restaurants and other German cultural aspects. Albeit quite loyal to this country, the German language and their treasured ethnicl aspects set them somewhat apart from all other Americans. However, as World War I began, many Americans felt that German-Americans were not loyal to this country, could not be trusted and could even be dangerous.

Throughout the U.S., certain individuals, groups, and politicians tried to rid the country of the German language, culture and influence. Germantown, Nebraska, was renamed Garland, East Germantown, Indiana, was changed to Pershing, Berlin, Iowa, became Lincoln, Berlin, Michigan, became Marne (after the Second Battle of the Marne in France). In June 1918, a Michigan congressman introduced a bill that would have required such name changes nationwide. Sauerkraut became liberty cabbage, hamburgers became liberty steaks, dachshunds became liberty pups, and German measles even became liberty measles. Some Americans even advocated ridding orchestras of music by Beethoven, Bach, and Mozart and banning all books written in German. Advertisements and poster were displayed like:

DO NOT VISIT THE SALOON BAKER - HE IS A GERMAN TRAITOR

Or, a poster would depict an German soldier bayoneting a little girl with the inscription: "Fuer GOTT, VATERLAND UND KOENIG. (For God, fatherland and King).

In 1918, South Dakota prohibited the use of German over the telephone and in public assemblies of three or more persons. The State of Iowa issued the following proclamation:

THE STATE OF IOWA

First, English should be and must be the only medium of instruction in public, private and other similar schools

Second, Conversation in public places, on trains and over the telephone should be in the English language.

Third, All public addresses should and must be in the English language

Fourth, Let those who cannot speak or understand the English language conduct their religious worship in their home.

Theodore Roosevelt endorsed Harding's "Babel Proclamation" stating: "America is a nation—not a polyglot boarding house. There can be but one loyalty—to the Stars and Stripes; one nationality—the American—and therefore only one language—the English language". President Woodrow Wilson spoke disapprovingly of "hyphenated Americans" whose loyalty he claimed was divided and a government official warned that "Every citizen must declare himself American--or traitor."

Commonly, German Americans were referred to as the "Huns" (after the Asian Huns who had destroyed ancient Rome). Some German Americans would lose their jobs and, for instance, Hans Kuhnwald, the famous concert master of the Cincinnati symphony orchestra, was removed from his post and detained. Mobs would even physically attack German Americans. According to Professor Katja Wüstenbecker, "citizens of German descent were dragged out of their homes at night and forced to kiss the flag or sing the national anthem". The most notorious case of mob action was the lynching of Robert Prager in Illinois in April 1918. Prager, a German native who had applied for American citizenship, was known to harbor socialist ideas and was suspected by his neighbors of stealing dynamite. Although this could not be proven, he was dragged out of town, stripped and hanged. This lynching caused outrage among many prominent Americans; nevertheless, court proceedings found the members of this mob not guilty.

Some German Americans reacted by overtly defending their loyalty to the United States. They would change their names or those of their businesses. Ironically, thousands of German Americans fought in the American Army during the end of World War I. They were under the command of the German American John J. Pershing whose family had changed their name from Pfoerschin to Pershing some time ago.

While this hysteria finally started to disappear, the damage had been done. The most pervasive damage was done to the German language and its use and education. And one could perhaps add to this to other foreign languages as well. Foreign languages were less taught or taught not at all in schools anymore. German news papers companies folded because they would not receive enough advertisements or would not be read out fear of being a traitor. Fortunately, the courts after 1925 declared these bans as illegal, German language could be used and taught again but the damage had been done. America lacked behind other Nations in fostering foreign language exposure in schools and universities (121–124). .

While this booklet talked up to now about the millions of hard working and honest Germans who came to this country, it should not be forgotten that among them was a small number of dishonest and ruthless individuals. The most known of them was Bruno Hauptmann who was born in Kamenz, Saxony. After a series of burglaries and break-ins in Germany, he escaped his trial and entered the United States illegally in 1923. Here, he was later convicted of having kidnapped and murdered the 20 month old child of Charles and Anne Lindbergh. While ransom money was paid, the child was never returned. The baby's body was found later in the woods just a few miles from the Lindbergh's home. The cause of death was determined to be a massive fracture of the skull. Albeit maintaining his innocence, he was convicted based on overwhelming circumstantial evidence. The chief evidence against Hauptmann was that some of the paid ransom money was found in his possession, the telephone number of the go-between was found to be written on a closet wall in Hauptmann's home, witnesses professed seeing him near the Lindbergh home and the ladder used to kidnap the baby contained a plank from Hauptmann's attic. He was electrocuted in 1936 and his crime was labeled as the "crime of the century". Albeit some historians are not sure if Hauptmann indeed was the kidnapper (150)

In summary, German immigration slowed considerably during this time and amounted to a few 100 000 immigrants. However, there was an influx of well of 100, 000 German speaking German Russians. With the opening of Ellis Island immigration policies changed marked. From now on, the Federal Government and not the individual States were in charge of immigration. Ellis Island proved very effective and processed usually up to 5,000 immigrants per day. Just before and during the war, a strong anti-sentiment against German Americans arose which resulted in the ban of the German language and provoked even physical assaults on German Americans. This occurred in spite of the fact that many German Americans fought and died for America in World War I. Finally, the ban on the use of the German language was overthrown by the courts but all these anti-German sentiments had caused some irreversible harm and the German language and culture never recovered completely.

THIRD REICH, WORLD WAR II, PRESENT

During this time, the emergence of the Third Reich and World War II shaped markedly the immigration of Germans to this country.

The Third Reich. After the end of World War I and the harsh Treaty of Versailles, Germany tried to establish a democracy called the Weimarer Republic (Weimar is a town in Germany). But serious economic conditions and political rivalries emerged immediately and both grew rapidly. In 1921, Germany suffered from a hyperinflation on a scale thought to be impossible by today's standards. A loaf of bread that had cost about 1-2 Marks but did cost around 160 Marks in1922 and then 200,000,000,000 Marks by late 1923. By November 1923, one US dollar was worth 4,210,500,000,000 German Marks. Fortunately, this inflation could be partially corrected by introducing a new currency in 1923.

To make matters worth, unemployment had risen sharply with over 6 million people being unemployed. This represented about 35-40 % of the entire work force. All these events led finally to the down fall of the Weimarer Republic and a political void. This was exploited by the "NSDAP" or "Nationalsozialistische Deutsche Arbeiter Partei" (National-socialistic German Workers Party) led by Adolf Hitler. Hitler proved to be an effective speaker and he promised an end to the current turmoil, more employment and restoration of the "good old" Germany". He also proved to be an effective organizer in channeling loyal party members into two "paramilitary" organizations: The "SA" ("Saalschutz" or Room Security wearing brown uniforms) and the SS ("Schutzstaffel" or Protective Echelon wearing black uniforms). These organizations started to terrorize members of or individuals sympathetic to other parties. With their help, the party was successful in several elections and finally managed to control a majority of seats in the "Deutsche Reichstag" (German Parliament). Adolf Hitler took office as Chancellor on January 30, 1933. Then a fire destroyed the German parliament which Hitler blamed on the communists (but might actually have been started by his own party members). Declaring this fire as a communistic plot to overthrow the government, he was given "emergency powers" by the Parliament which he never gave up. On July 14, 1933, the Nazi Party was formally declared to be the only political party in Germany. Soon prominent members of the communistic and social-democratic parties disappeared and were detained in newly established concentration camps. Individual unions were suppressed and merged into a government controlled labor organization. After the death of the then president von Hindenburg, Hitler assumed the title of Führer (leader) und Reichskanzler (chancellor). On August 1935, a plebiscite confirmed his new office with 88 percent of 43,529,710 votes cast (mostly coerced by his party members). Democracy had died and an evil dictatorship had emerged in Germany. From there on the State – or Hitler – controlled fully the lives of all German citizens. There were only government controlled newspapers and radio stations, all news were government controlled and foreign news papers were outlawed. Germans either joined the party voluntarily or involuntarily (just to keep their jobs, for instance) or would fade into the background keeping their mouths shut and following the party's laws, rules and regulations. Germans were told that they are members of the Arian race which is superior to all other races. The ideal Arian was supposed to be slim, blond and tall. This immediately gave rise to the following joke in Germany (which, of course, could only be told among very trusted friends): "The true Arian is slim like Goering (Field marshal and later vice chancellor who was grossly overweight), tall like Goebels (Propaganda minister and quite small with a limp) and blond like Hitler (who had black hair).

Unfortunately, just to keep quiet was not good enough for the German Jewish population which actually felt very much to be German and many German Jews had fought bravely and had died in the First World War for Germany. Most Germans did not – at least openly – express anti-Semitic feelings. The author remembers two of his teachers in his "High school" who had been Jewish – and nobody knew or cared about it unless they later lost their jobs and were denounced by the local Nazi government as Jewish. The author also remembers quite well that a common saying among Germans went as follows: if you need a good Doctor or Lawyer, go to a Jewish one. And even most Jews did not take the anti-semitic words of the party serious in the beginning.

The persecution started with the Nuremberg (Nuernberg) laws. They were designed by Adolf Hitler and approved by his Nazi Party at a convention in Nuremberg in 1935. The Reichsbürgergesetz (Law of Reich Citizen) deprived Jews of German citizenship, and designated them "subjects of the state." The "Gesetz zum Schutze des Deutschen Blutes und der Deutschen Ehre ("Law for the Protection of German Blood and German Honour"), usually called simply the Blutschutzgesetz ("Blood Protection Law"), forbade marriage or sexual relations between Jews and "citizens of German or kindred blood. Of interest is the opinion of George Kareski, the chairman of the German State Zionists at this time, who was interviewed on the Nuremberg Laws by Goebbels's magazine "Der Angriff" (The Attack). Kareski said that the Nuremberg Laws fulfilled old Jewish demands. For example, the separation of German and Jewish nationality, the establishment of schools for Jewish students only, nurturing and supporting a specific Jewish culture, and above all the state prohibition of mixed marriages, which in any case Jewish law did not permit. It is not clear if this was his personal opinion or if he had to say so to save his own life and to avoid more harm for his fellow Jews.

Unfortunately, it did not stop there. From now on Jews were dismissed from their jobs, their businesses were curtailed and finally confiscated and in on night – "the night of the broken glass" – many Jewish shops were looted and damaged. Then came the imprisonment of Jewish individuals in Germany and occupied countries ending with the mass murder in specified extermination camps. It has been estimated that more than 6 million Jews were murdered in these camps as well in other places as well.

World War II. Then World War II erupted. This war involved up to 30 countries with the principal countries being the "Axis": Germany, Italy and Japan—and the "Allies" : France, Great Britain, Soviet Union and the United States. It was basically the result of Hitler's expansion policies or his ambitions to expand Germany's territory to the East. In Europe, it started when Germany invaded Poland on September 1, 1939 and Great Britain and France responded by declaring war on Germany on September 3. The war between the U.S.S.R. and Germany began on June 22, 1941, with the German invasion of the Soviet Union. On December 11, 1941,

Germany declared war on the USA since its partner Japan had done so just before.

In the beginning, Germany was quite successful by employing the "Blitzkieg" (lightening war) strategy. It quite quickly conquered

Poland and France. It also occupied a number of smaller countries like Holland, Belgium and Norway. It was also successful against Russia and the German troops reached the outskirts of Moscow until a brutal winter forced them to stop. From there on, German troops were forced to retreat and suffered its biggest defeat in the battle around Stalingrad. With the Allies landing at Normandy Beach on June 6, 1944, Germany now had to fight on two fronts exceeding its capabilities. Soon Allied troops both from the East and West entered German soil and moved towards Berlin. After the fall of Berlin and the suicide of Hitler, Germany surrendered unconditionally to the Allies in May of 1945. After 12 years, the Third Reich had collapsed and Germany lay in ruins. Finally, the Paris Peace Treaties were signed on February, 10, 1947. The treaties allowed the defeated Axis powers to begin as sovereign states again but also demanded payment of war reparations, commitment to minority rights and territorial adjustments (the latter resulted, for instance,in the loss of some German land in the east to Poland). The treaties also obliged the various states to hand over accused war criminals to the Allied powers for war crime trials.

The war in the Pacific began on December 7/8, 1941, when Japan attacked the American naval base at Pearl Harbor and other American territories throughout Asia. The Japanese were quite successful in the Pacific after their surprise attack. But losing afterwards some major battles including the one at Midway, Japan also had to retreat. After the detonation of two nuclear weapons over Hiroshima and Nagasaki, Japan surrendered on August 15, 1945 and World War II had finally ended. It is perhaps of interest that Nagasaki was not the atom bomb's original target but it was the City of Kokura. However, clouds covered this city and the American plane made several passes over the city and reported that they could not locate the target aim. Thus, the mission was changed to Nagasaki. Ironically, clouds determined that lives in Kokura were saved while lives in Nagasaki were lost.

The death toll of the war is estimated to be about 40 to 50 million soldiers and civilians. This makes it the bloodiest military conflict in history (125-129).

Germany today. After 1949, there existed 2 Germanys. One was the "Bundesrepublik Deutschland" (Federal Republic of Germany) or West Germany which was formally established as a separate and independent nation on May 23, 1949. It covered the former British, France and American occupied sectors. This led to the establishment of the "Deutsche Demokratische Republik" (German Democratic Republic) or East Germany which covered the area of the Russian controlled sector. Both Germanys had a rough start. Cities lay in ruins and factories were defunct. Unemployment was high and food was scarce. West Germany received help from America through the Marshal Plan and was able to rebuild the country relatively quickly with a free economy in an orderly fashion without the turmoil which had occurred after the end of World War I. East Germany, in contrast, suffered from Russian domination and exploitation and was not able to rebuild a functioning and lasting communistic economy. Thus, the discontent of their people with the communistic dictatorship and the failing economy led to its collapse and both countries united on October 3, 1990. German is now one of the most stable Democracies and one of the wealthiest nations in Europe. At present, there are few reasons to emigrate from Germany (128-130).

German American and the Third Reich. In America, many German Americans were quite impressed what they learned about the upswing and recovery of Germany under the reigns of Hitler and the Nazi party. This was reinforced by a well planned propaganda campaign from Goebels, the propaganda minister of the Third

Reich. This led to the formation of Nazi friendly German American groups which eventually merged into the "Bund" (Union). It was led by Fritz Kuhn who was a strong Nazi sympathizer. He had to flee Germany due to the fact that he had embezzled money from his employer. He went to Mexico first and then came to America where he became a naturalized American Citizen. The Bund supported Hitler's policies in particular its anti-Semitism. It was most active between 1936 and 1939 where it might have been 20 000 members strong. It operated two camps modeled after German Nazi camps with uniforms and Nazi salutes. The camps flew two flags: the American Flag and the Nazi Flag side by side. It staged several rallies with the rally in New York in 1939 to be the largest attracting about 20 000 people. Banners hanging from the balconies proclaimed "Stop Jewish Domination of Christian America." When government officials began investigating the Bund and looked into its finances they found that the self styled "American Fuehrer" Kuhn had been embezzling money from the organization. He was prosecuted, convicted in late 1939, sent to prison and deported in 1945. The bund fell slowly apart after his arrest. It is interesting, that members following Nazi ideology nevertheless considered themselves "true Americans".

During WWII, the United States feared that some Nazi sympathizers might actually be a threat to the security of the USA. Thus, the American government examined the cases of suspicious German Americans or recently immigrated Germans but detained relatively few in internment camps run by the Department of Justice. This number is estimated to be about 2000. This is considerably less than the about 100,000 Japanese who were placed in these internment camps.

However, the fear that national or ethnic Germans would side with the Nazis in Germany and commit destructive acts in America was not totally unfounded. The historian Professor Ross uncovered the fascinating story of how some Nazis from Germany indeed infiltrated America and recruited sympathetic Americans to carry out plans to subvert the government, destroy military installations and to kill Jewish individuals. These plans were foiled by the Jewish lawyer Lewis who created a network of spies to stop these acts successfully before any major damage or loss of lives did occur. Thus, any major destructive actions never materialized.

Another case was the Rumrich spy case of 1938 (as outlined in the FBI History). It all began when a naturalized U.S. citizen named Rumrich who had been recruited by the German intelligence was arrested by the New York Police because he had been impersonating the Secretary of State in order to get blank U.S. passports. Rumrich confessed that he was acting on behalf of Nazi agents. He was also willing to provide the names of 10 to 15 spies working for Germany. The FBI unprepared for such an espionage problems did not handle the case well and only a few spies got convicted while most of the more important ones did manage to escape. However, this case made the FBI aware of this security problem and it started to reform and greatly improve its espionage training and operations.

Public opinion against Germans immigrants and German Americans was much more moderated than it had been during World War I. Direct assaults were few but they did occur. One German American wrote:" Some of my grandparents friends turned on them because we are of Germany ancestry. My uncle was killed in WWII and one woman said he deserved to die because he was German". However, the public was more and perhaps equally divided in the question if America should intervene and join the war or if America should stay neutral. President Franklin Roosevelt led the interventionist charge, while aviator Charles Lindbergh became an unofficial leader of the isolationist movement. But this was quickly solved after both Japan and Germany declared war on the USA and now both sides had to defend the country. Lindbergh and many others including many German Americans joined the army and bravely fought and died for America (131-137).

German immigration before 1945. The years after World War I and the Third Reich and World War II affected markedly the influx of German immigrants in particular that of Jewish individuals.

At the beginning of the Great Depression in 1930, President Herbert Hoover issued instructions not to admit immigrants "likely to become a public charge". Furthermore, sentiment among the unemployed Americans against immigrants was strong because American workers feared that these immigrants would compete with them for the few jobs available. In 1933, there was also the fear that German immigrants might aid the Third Reich but this fear turned out to be unsupported. In this year, only 8,220 quota immigrants arrived in the United States, a ninety-five percent decrease in immigration compared to the years prior. Albeit President Roosevelt liberalized these laws a bit but this did not markedly affect the influx of immigrants.

However, this changed before and after 1933. The number of immigrants seeking asylum in America increased markedly due to the escape of Jewish individuals from the ever worsening conditions for Jews in Nazi Germany. In the beginning, the Nazi government actually encouraged Jews to emigrate. However, after the "Kristallnacht" (literally "crystal night" or better known as the night of the broken glass) in 1938, it became quite difficult because now Jews were imprisoned and send to concentration and later extermination camps. However, immigration into America was quite difficult and only a few succeeded while a large number was unsuccessful and many of these would wind up in extermination camps. A variety of reasons were responsible for this dilemma.

The American government did not do enough to save Jewish lives from extermination. Politicians and government officials just followed the law which restricted the number of immigrants from Germany without extending its number due to the horrors these Jewish people faced in the Third Reich. American law at this time made very little distinction between refugees forced to flee their country due to persecution and immigrants seeking a better life. Furthermore government officials from the State Department to the FBI to President Franklin Roosevelt himself argued that refugees posed a serious threat to national security. Yet today, historians believe these concerns about refugee spies were blown far out of proportion. Even a group of Jewish congressmen met but decided not to introduce any new legislation to expand immigration to aid Jewish refugees. Furthermore, public anti-immigration sentiment remained strong—in 1938, only 23% of Americans were in favor of expanding the immigration quota of German refugees and about 70% responded with a "No" to the question "Should we allow a larger number of Jewish exiles from Germany to come to the States to live". Several other bills were then introduced to aid these refugees but none passed. The only significant attempt to pass a law to aid refugees came in 1939, when Democratic Senator Robert Wagner of New York and Republican Congresswoman Edith Rogers of Massachusetts introduced legislation in both houses of Congress that would allow 20,000 German refugee children under the age of 14 into the country over a period of two years outside of the immigration quotas. Unfortunately, this legislation never made it out of committee for a vote. All this proofed disastrous for many German Jews.

A case in point is he ship "St Louis". In May 1939, the ship sailed from Germany to Havana with 937 passengers onboard most of them being Jewish, The Cuban government refused the ship to dock and when it tried to sail to America, the USA government also disallowed the ship to dock because they did not have the appropriate immigration papers. Thus, the ship was forced to return and England, France and Belgium accepted some passengers with the rest being discharged to Germany where later on about 250 of them were murdered in various concentration camps. This episode has been made into a movie called "Ship of Fools".

The number which could have been saved is illustrated by the data showing that, for instance, 1938, there were 125,000 applicants lined up outside US consulates hoping to obtain 27,000 visas under the existing immigration quota. By June 1939, the number of applicants had increased to over 300,000. Most visa applicants were unsuccessful and had to remain in Germany. One Jewish immigrant wrote:" The United States did everything it could at that time, under President Roosevelt, to keep as many Jews out as possible. My family and I actually became Republicans because we were so appalled at the way Roosevelt closed the doors to the Jewish immigrants."

A second reason was that the Nazi government allowed Jews to emigrate but placed some restrictions on this offer. The Nazi government required Jews to have a valid visa for the country they wished to immigrate to and to possess a valid paid-for voyage ticket. As outlined above, most countries including America had quotas that limited the number of immigrants. Furthermore, many countries including the USA required visa seekers to enter only if they were able to support themselves. This presented often a major problem since many Jews had been driven by the Nazi government into poverty. They were first dismissed from their jobs, then property and possessions were confiscated and Germans were forbidden to buy from Jewish stores. Often their apartments were ransacked and valuables, art and other precious items were confiscated. Thus, many

Jews just could not afford the cost of the voyage or the voyage to freedom.

Here, a number of Jewish organizations as well as some Christian Churches collected money and prepaid the ships' ticket for some German Jews. Despite the varied and courageous efforts to rescue thousands of their co-religionists, they could do little to save millions of European Jews from the Nazi genocide. Money was scarce and soon the coffers were empty. However, it has also been stated by Jewish historians that American Jews could have helped more and could have prevented thousands of deaths.

There were also some individuals who helped German Jews to immigrate. For instance, the American Raymond Geist who was Consul in Berlin from 1929 to 1939 made it known that American families could adopt German-Jewish children, thus ensuring that these families' resources would keep such rescued children from becoming public burdens. Geist himself shepherded a program that by 1938 had brought approximately 350 German-Jewish children to the U.S. With a name like Geist (meaning Ghost) he must have been of German descent.

Furthermore, arriving in this country often provided the immigrants with freedom but also with unforeseen economic challenges. Most of them arrived with only a few suit cases, a little bit of money and perhaps some jewelry or gold. They tried to find shelter with relatives or friends if they could find them and if they were welcome. They might even have lived on the street at first and earned a living as peddlers. Some tried to open small stores. Life was extremely hard for many. One story describes the life of a former respected and wealthy lawyer from Vienna, Austria, who managed to come to New York. On arrival, he was assigned the job of "houseman" in a Jewish fraternity house and paid a minimum of wages. He was constantly insulted, humiliated because he spoke accented English and ridiculed because of his beard. His life was made miserable until he succeeded in gaining an academic appointment.

In can be estimated that between 1930 and 1939 bout about 90.000 Jews were lucky and where granted asylum in the United States while about 90 000 immigrated to South America mostly Argentina, Chile and Brazil. Smaller numbers went to Palestine, Switzerland, China and other non German occupied countries.

Because of its anti-Semitic policies, Germany lost many noted Jewish scientists which helped to advance American Science greatly while it hurt German Science significantly. As a matter of fact, among those immigrated scientists were twelve Nobel Prize winning scientists with seven of these being Jewish.

This exodus of German Jews is one of the ironies of history. Hitler's hate of the Jewish race might actually have contributed to his down fall. Many Jewish men, whose fathers had fought bravely for Germany in World War I, might have again fought for Germany in World War II. Now they were fighting against Germany. In particular, this was the case with the loss of Jewish theoretical and nuclear scientists. At this time, both Germany and America were working on the development of the atom bomb. While Germany was ahead in the beginning, it can be posited that these Jewish scientists might have eventually given the Third Reich the Atom bomb and perhaps victory. However, losing these brilliant scientists, set Germany way back but benefitted greatly America. These scientists like Albert Einstaein, Hans Bethe, John von Neumann, Leo Szilard, James Franck, Edward Teller, Rudolf Peierls, Dieter Gruen, Klaus Fuchs and Enrico Fermi all came to America and many began working on the Manhattan Project or the development of the atom bomb. This project succeeded with the manufacturing of "Little Boy" and "Fat Man", the two bombs dropped in Japan. While causing devastating damage and killing about 500,000 people immediately and delayed by radiation induced diseases, most historians feel that it shortened the war and saved millions of lives if the war had continued (138-142, 151,152, 158, 159).

Last, here, are few examples of famous German born immigrants:

Arnold Schwarzenegger born in Austria (which later became part of Germany) went from body builder to movie star and finally Governor of California.

Albert Einstein, Nobel Prize winner, was born in Ulm, Baden-Wuertenberg. He was teaching at the University of Berlin, when he started to fear for his life because of being Jewish. Interestingly, his visa was denied by the American government because he was believed to be a communist. This was followed by a public outcry and the visa was issued. He left Germany and took a position at the Institute for Advanced Study in New Jersey. Several years later, Einstein wrote to then president Franklin D. Roosevelt about the looming threat of German Nazism and encouraged him to start work on an atomic bomb—a letter that is said to be largely responsible for the creation of the Manhattan Project and the completion of the atomic bomb project.

Actor Bruce Willis was born in Idar-Oberstein, Palanate, to an American father and a German mother. Shortly after his birth, the family moved to the States. In school, Bruce stuttered and was nick-named "Buck Buck". To help with his stuttering, he joined the Drama club which later on led to a career in acting.

Henry Kissinger was born in Fuerth, Bavaria as Heinz Alfred Kissinger. Due to his Jewish heritage, the family left for the States. He served in the American Army and graduated summa cum laude with a PhD from Harvard in Political Science. He co-founded the Center for International Affairs and wrote a book titled: *Nuclear Weapons and Foreign Policy*. He was appointed National Security Advisor and later on U.S. Secretary of State under President Nixon.

Marie Magdalene "Marlene" Dietrich was born in Schoeneberg (now a district of Berlin). After choosing an acting career, she stared in several German films. After an offer from Hollywood, she moved to the States and became one of the highest paid actresses (138-142, 151,152).

German Immigration after 1945 until now. After the war, there were a number of changes in the American immigration laws. The most important one was the Immigration and Nationality Act (or Hart-Celler Act) of 1965. The new law abolished the discriminatory national origins quota system established in the 1924 Immigration Act.15 The cap for the total quota for the eastern hemisphere was set at 170,000. The law also imposed a ceiling of 120,000 for the western hemisphere with no limits for individual nations. A new preference system was introduced, as well as a labor certification program.

The number of German immigrants slowly declined from 1950 to present time as the economic situation in Germany grew stronger and people could start to make a good living.. During this time span about 300,000 Germans immigrated to America.

Among them were "immigrants" who were somehow coerced to come to America. At the end of World War II, a covert operation later named "paperclip", brought about 1600 German rocket scientists and engineers with their families to the USA. Among them was Wernher von Braun with about 100 of his closest associates. This transfer to the States had to occur quickly because the Russians also would have liked to bring this same group to Russia. They were moved to the U.S. Army Ordnance Corps test site at Fort Bliss, Texas and White Sands, New Mexico, where they were employed to first experiment with captured V-2 rockets for high-altitude research purposes. Later, the team was moved to various places to develop the Redstone, Jupiter-C, Juno, and Pershing missiles and the space launch vehicles Saturn I and others. The engineering success of each rocket in the Saturn class of space boosters, which contained millions of individual parts, remains unparalleled in rocket history. Each of them was launched successfully, on time and met all safe-performance requirements. The Saturn 1 became the basic test vehicle that led to the development of the Saturn V that carried men to the Moon for Project Apollo. Many of these individuals later became citizens and stayed in the country.

Wernher von Braun was born in Wirsik, East Prussia, but his family moved to Berlin shortly thereafter. He did not do well in school, in particularly with physics and mathematics. But reading " Die Rakete zu den Planetenräumen" (The Rocket into Interplanetary Space) by rocket pioneer, Hermann Oberth, awakened and changed him. Frustrated by his inability to understand the mathematics, he applied himself until he finally mastered his short comings. During his graduate studies, he became a member of the German Society for Space Travel. After graduation, he joined the Rocket Developmental Station of the Third Reich where he later became the technical Director. Here, he worked on the development of ballistic missiles which finally led to the development of the "**V**ergeltungswaffe 1 and 2 or V1 and V2" (**V**engeance weapons V1 and V2). These weapons were basically rocket propelled large bombs. They were mostly aimed at London where a V2 impact could destroy an entire city block. To protect the manufacturing of these rockets from allied bombings, they were finally built in tunnels in a mountain near Nordhausen.

What is less known – and what von Braun had known – was the inhuman treatment of the workforce in the V1 and V2 production tunnels. This workforce was comprised of forced laborers from occupied countries as well as prisoners from various concentration camps. He sometimes even visited these camps to select new workers. These "workers" worked and slept in these cool tunnels without being provided some warm clothing. Toilets were metal barrels with a large hole cut into the top. Food was just enough to prevent them from dying of starvation albeit many did die. If a rocket would later malfunction, workers from this station were executed. It has been estimated that about 12000 workers were worked to death in these tunnels. If he would not have moved to America, he most likely would have been tried as a war criminal (143,144).

A second wave occurred between 1950 and about 1970. Many of these immigrants at this time were mostly scientists and physicians. This was partially due to the Russians launching Sputnik and America felt that it was falling behind in the space race but also in science and medicine in general. In addition, America experienced a shortage of physicians at this time. Germany, on the other hand, had many scientists who had difficulties finding work since there were not enough laboratories and the main interest of the German government was to rebuild houses, factories and the transport systems as quickly as possible. Similarly, with the return of many German army physicians into civilian life, there was a surplus of physicians and many young physicians were not able to establish their own offices. Thus, a number of USA programs was established to entice German scientists and physicians to come short term or long term to the States. Many of these married scientists and physicians decided then to stay in this country for good. Similarly, many single individuals would meet and marry an American mate and also would stay in this country. The author was one of these scientists who came with his wife to the States and both decided to become citizens.

However, a new wave of Germans is now coming to the Southern States on a temporary basis. These Germans buy properties and come only in the winter months to escape the dreary winters in Germany and to bath in the warm southern sun. They can obtain a special visa which allows them to stay for 6 months per year (albeit their property taxes have to be paid for 12 months). Such temporary Germans can account in some counties in Florida for up to 20% of all residents in the winter months.

In summary, the great depression in 1930 tried to discourage immigration since American workers feared the competition from the immigrants for the few jobs available. The Third Reich with its anti-Jewish laws and later their mass extermination forced many Jews to flee Germany and German occupied countries and to immigrate to America. While this country accepted a fair number of Jewish refugees, the government under Roosevelt and some Jewish organizations helped but could have done more and could have saved more lives. Among these immigrants were a number of nuclear scientists who later significantly helped in developing the atom bomb. After the war, America moved a large group of German rocket specialists under the leadership of Wernher von Braun to America to have them work on its space program. Here, they helped America considerably to be successful in many of its space adventures. Many of the immigrated Jewish scientists and physicians made American Science a leader in the world as evidenced by the large number of Nobel prizes awarded.

CITIZEN OR RESIDENT

After arrival in this country, immigrants had to make a choice to become a citizen or to remain a resident. In general, all citizens and residents enjoyed certain rights and privileges equally, however, other privileges like participation in local governments, acting on a jury, and the right later on to vote is only allowed a citizen. The qualifications to become a citizen in America varied from time to time but can perhaps best be divided into British Colonial Times (excluding Spanish or Mexican controlled territories) and the United States of America.

British Colonial Times. In the very beginning, the first settlers did not worry about this decision. If they came from England, they remained English citizens and, thus, were full subjects of the English King. Immigrants from other countries usually remained as residents albeit often not obtaining the same legal rights as English citizens. As the number of Non-English residents increased, the English Parliament initiated some proceedings in 1659 indicating how these foreign persons could become English citizens. This was one way to bind the colonies closer to England. Soon ambiguities arose questioning if naturalization should be granted by England alone or by the Colonial Authorities. Soon, both authorities started to make their own laws and to issue their individual citizenship papers. Among the different ways to become an English citizen was the private naturalization before the English Parliament which afforded the highest legal status. This process was granted only to people with high moral character, it was quite expensive costing about 50 pounds at this time and it was also exclusive. It was granted to certain Christian individuals only and not to Catholics and certain non-Christian groups.

In 1663, The Linen Cloth Act modified some of these guidelines and favored certain professional groups for naturalization which were in dire need by the Colonies. This was followed by some other laws which, like the Foreign Protestant Naturalization Act of 1708, would allow, for instance, French Protestants (Huguenots) and certain other Christian groups to become citizens. In 1740 Parliament responded with a more liberal and enlightened policy that greatly eased and broadened the ability of aliens in the American colonies to become naturalized subjects of Britain. The Plantation act of 1740 did not require applicants to travel to London but aliens could now locally apply for naturalization within the colonies so long as they had resided there for seven years or more, without being absent more than two consecutive months. It also reduced the fee to 2 Shillings but required the applicant to take an oath of allegiance to the Crown and to profess their Protestant belief in open court. It was still difficult for Catholics or Jews to obtain citizenship. In most cases, individual judges would be the persons granting citizenship.

Next, individual Colonies developed their own naturalization laws often with differing requirements and sometimes also outside of common English law. However, each colony could only create citizenships within its border and not beyond. New Hampshire followed strictly the laws of the English Parliament while other colonies deviated more or less from them. Conservative New England kept its Colony selectively more English. Massachusetts required any ship entering its ports to provide a passenger list, and later prohibited the importation of poor, infirm or vicious individuals. Connecticut started to demand oath of allegiance from all strangers spending time within its borders. In Virginia, naturalization laws included a preamble that extolled the advantage of inviting other persons to reside in the colony. It also granted the governor or Chief-in-Command the power to naturalize foreigners. South Carolina attracted alien applicants through naturalization laws that granted them the same rights of natural-born Englishmen while prohibiting the collection of monies for debts contracted prior to the applicant coming to the colony. Pennsylvania provided its own general law for naturalization that gave full rights to aliens who had resided in the colony for less than the required seven years. New York and Pennsylvania both exempted persons with conscientious scruples against oaths, which included Quakers, from the requirement to swear allegiance during naturalization. These individual powers, however, were severely curtailed and equalized by the British Parliament in 1773.

In spite of all of these naturalization opportunities, many non-English persons did not become naturalized. Albeit officially deprived of certain privileges, colonies often overlooked the law and offered such individuals nevertheless the same rights (161,162).

The United States. After the war of independence and the establishment of the United States of America, these procedures now changed completely. Nevertheless, immigration was still tied to the needs of the United States. If need for foreigners was great, immigration of such individuals was facilitated while if there appeared to be no need, immigration was curtailed.

From now on, citizenship of the United States entails specific rights, duties and benefits in the United States. Citizenship is understood as a "right to have rights" since it serves as a foundation of fundamental rights derived from and protected by the Constitution and laws of the United States.

The Citizenship Clause of the Constitution's 1868 Fourteenth Amendment states basically that there are two ways to become an American citizen.

One is through primary birth rights such as being born within the territorial limits of the United States or being born outside the US territory to two or one Parents holding American citizenship. However, in the beginning, there was an exclusion in that such citizenship could not be enjoyed by black people or "Negros". Such individuals could become State citizens but not citizens of the United States. The decision was finally reversed by the Civil Rights Act of 1865.

The second way is to apply for citizenship if an individual has a different nationality. This is referred to as Naturalization and will be explored in more detail. This process involves the application for citizenship by an individual, its processing and finally its approval or disapproval by a specific government agency.

It started out that the process of naturalization was performed by officials from individual states albeit under some federal guidance. There were also a number of changes implemented over the years. One part of the process which was changed frequently was the residence requirement. In 1790, this changed and the federal government assumed complete responsibility by establishing uniform rules for all States including a 2 year residence requirement. Interestingly, residence requirements were soon raised to 5 years and then to 14 years in 1798 but were reduced again to years 4 years later on.

Similarly, it was felt by many judges (naturalization was handled by State courts) that applicants for naturalization should have some knowledge of history and the government of their chosen country. Since naturalization was handled by the courts, judges would do the questioning. As can be expected, their requirements must have differed quite a lot and often were used to facilitate or to deny an application. The questions generally involved various aspects of history and civics. In 1906, the federal Bureau of Naturalization began to oversee and standardize naturalization proceedings nationally. It offered naturalization officials test questions which should be used to access an applicant's knowledge.

Today, the standardized test consists of two parts:

1. The English test with the three components of reading, writing and speaking.
2. Civic test which is concerned with American history and government.

Most German immigrants today eventually will apply for citizenship to stay permanently in this country.

However, a person can stay in this country without becoming a citizen This could be the result of many factors but most likely a combination of some. by obtaining a "green card" or a permanent Resident card. Green cards got their nickname because they were green from 1946 to 1964. These holders enjoy all the privileges of a citizen and can even serve in the army except they cannot vote or serve on a jury. At present, there are about 13 million green card holders in the USA and about 9 million are eligible to become citizens. However, the green card can be revoked if such an individual is convicted of any criminal act. German green card holders are mostly individuals who are send from their German companies to the States to direct or work for their subsidiaries(163-173).

Passports. Another document necessary to identify a citizen is the passport. Passports were already issued shortly after the Establishment of the United States and Benjamin Franklin carried one on his mission to France. Early American passports were modeled after the French passports. In 1789, the State Department, States and some Cities did issue passports. Passports not issued by the State Department, however, were often not recognized by other nations. During this period, the United States did not require a passport to enter or exit the country. At the start of World War I passports became more standardized and the typical layout of today's passport originated in 1926. It identifies a naturalized American since it displays the country of his or her origin. Today, it is required to present a passport when leaving or entering the United States (173).

In summary, during Colonial times, the only "true" citizens were The English either born as such or naturalized later on. However, naturalization was exclusive in that Catholics had almost no chance to become an English citizen. Most non-English immigrants remained non-citizens at this time. The creation of the United States determined that citizenship can also be obtained by naturalization and passing a test. Most German immigrants do apply for citizenship. Permanent stay in the states can also be obtained through the green card which is most often used by individuals who work for German companies here at their subsidiaries.

OUTLOOK

The future of German immigrations is uncertain but speculations can be made nevertheless. There are basically two scenarios to consider.

One scenario is that the economic and cultural state of Germany continues to be good and acceptable to most Germans. In this case, immigration will only occur at a very low level.

Another scenario is that the conditions of today's Germany change to the worse in the years to come. In this case, immigration will most likely increase.

Such a worsening could be result of many factors. One possibility is a decline of ethnic Germans and domination by Islamic Germans. While this does not exist today, but certain indications could predict such an outcome. First, it is estimated that Germany has now a total population of about 80 million citizens of which about 12 million are muslin immigrants. This means that 15.8% of the German population is not ethnic. Since it can be expected that this immigration will increase since there will be family reunions as well as new arrivals. Furthermore, the birth rate of ethnic Germans is around 1.6 while the birth rate of migrant women is about 2.2. These figures are the average number of children born to one woman. If a population has a number of 2.1, it will remain at the same level. If these figures are below or above 2.1 than the population will decrease or increase over time. Thus, the number of ethnic Germans is decreasing while that of the migrant population is increasing. This is supported by a Pew study which predicts that in 2100 Christians had better to get ready to live in a world in which they are likely to be a minority. Second, another problem is the surge in crime mostly committed by immigrants from the mid eastern countries According to the German Interior Ministry, surveys have shown a major increase in violent crimes including a 14.3% rise in murders and manslaughters, a 12.7% rise in rapes and sexual assaults, and a 9.9% increase in serious assaults over the previous years. The figures also indicate that illegal immigrants, refugees and asylum seekers committed more than half of these crimes in spite of being a very small minority at present. Interior Minister Thomas de Maiziere called the increase in migrant crime '"unacceptable" and vowed to expel illegal migrants who committed crimes. What is more worrisome is the fact that these figures might actually have been manipulated by the government. They have been made to look better to help Chancellor Merkel to squash Anti- Immigration sentiments. Third, most Islamic immigrants based on their cultural backgrounds and religious beliefs only superficially assimilate into the German culture while strongly clinging to their religious and cultural roots. Their religious beliefs are incompatible with the German Christian beliefs where Religion and State are separate entities. The Islamic religion, however, combines both with religion being the dominant force. Studies also find that Muslims are stronger believers than are Christians with Mosques over- flowing at services while Churches are only half full. This fear is supported by recent events in France where certain Arabic neighborhoods actually substituted Islamic for French law. The French president was forced to intervene in order to prevent such "Islamic separatism".

One European observer, Igor Pshenichnikov, warns if these current trends continue, Germany as we know it now, will cease to exist within this century. Ethnic Germans will be in the minority and will be outnumbered by Muslims. These circumstances might entice or even force many ethnic Germans to leave Germany and to immigrate to the United States which could produce another wave of immigrants.

However, these scenarios also depend on America at this time and if this country is worse off than Germany or if it can offer opportunities which would not be available in Germany and would be inviting to Germans. It has been predicted for the years 2060 and thereafter that in America whites will represent about 40 %, Hispanics about 35 % and Blacks about 15% and others about 10% of the entire population. Religious diversity for these years is projected to be about 55% Christians, 2 % Muslims, 13% other religions and 30% unaffiliated. If religion plays a role in the decision to immigrate, America again would be the country to go to for Christian German citizens. (157,158,172-175). .

In summary, immigration can continue at the current slow pace but can increase or decrease dramatically depending on the future economic, cultural and religious conditions in Germany and the USA.

REFERENCES

1   https://statisticalatlas.com/United-States/Ancestry .

2   https://www.loc.gov/rr/european/imde/germchro.html

3   https://www.smithsonianmag.com/smart-news/humans-colonized-americas-along-coast-not-through-ice-180960103/

4   http://nationalhumanitiescenter.org/pds/amerbegin/settlement/settlement.htm

5   https://en.wikipedia.org/wiki/History_of_North_America

6   http://www.sci-news.com/archaeology/cerutti-mastodon-site-humans-north-america-04815.html

7   https://www.history.com/topics/exploration/exploration-of-north-america

8   https://georgiahistory.com/education-outreach/online-exhibits/featured-historical-figures/hernando-de-soto/early-spanish-exploration-in-north-america/

9   http://www.germanheritage.com/Publications/Jamestown/first.html

10 https://www.britannica.com/place/Jamestown-Colony/The-Starving-Time-and-near-abandonment-1609-11

11 https://www.history.com/topics/colonial-america/plymouth#section_2

12 www.historyworld.net/wrldhis/PlainTextHistories.asp?.

13 https://www.britannica.com/biography/Martin-Luther

14 https://www.britannica.com/event/Diet-of-Worms-Germany-1521

15 http://www.historyworld.net/wrldhis/PlainTextHistories.asp?ParagraphID=fyt#ixzz6L1ilt9SK

16 http://www.lordsandladies.org/serfs.htm

17 https://www.christianity.com/church/church-history/timeline/1501-1600/german-peasant-revolt-11629931.html and https://www.britannica.com/event/Thirty-Years-War

18 http://www.revisionist.net/hysteria/early-settlers.html

19 http://www.germanheritage.com/Publications/Jamestown/sawmill.html

20 http://nationalhumanitiescenter.org/pds/amerbegin/settlement/settlement.htm

21 https://www.biography.com/political-figure/peter-minuit

22 https://www.history.com/this-day-in-history/first-mennonites-arrive-in-america

23 https://www.germantown-tn.gov/live/about-the-city/history

24 http://genealogytrails.com/penn/philadelphia/phlhistgtown.html

25 http://www.meetinghouse.info/early-history-of-the-germantown-congregation.html

26 https://www.muelheim-ruhr.de/cms/germantown_-_muelheimer_auswanderer_in_amerika2.html

27 https://amishamerica.com/first-amish-community-north-america/

28 https://www.discoverlancaster.com/amish/history-beliefs/

29 https://amishamerica.com/history/

30 Hermann Hage: Amische Mennoniten in Bayern. Regensburg 2009, ISBN 978-3-939112-45-7

31 http://sites.rootsweb.com/~GENHOME/imm1a.htm

32 https://www.cob-net.org/antietam/dunkers.htm

33 https://www.ucc.org/about-us_hidden-histories_the-schwenkfelders

34 http://old.artintheage.com/pa-schwenkfelder-heritage-relics-a-brief-history/#.Xqck12hKg-E

35 http://dianestokoe.com/waldensians/waldensian_01.pdf

36 https://en.wikipedia.org/wiki/History_of_the_Moravian_Church#Early_history:_the_Czech_background

37 https://www.britannica.com/place/Bohemia

38 https://moraviansinnorthcarolina.weebly.com/moravian-history.html

39 http://www.eyewitnesstohistory.com/passage.htm

40 http://www.lookbackward.com/migration.htm

41 https://familypedia.wikia.org/wiki/Immigrant_Ships_To_America/First_Families/Winthrop_Fleet

42 http://homepages.rootsweb.com/~brobst/chronicles/chap2.htm

43 https://www.britannica.com/biography/William-Penn-English-Quaker-leader-and-colonist

44 http://homepages.rootsweb.com/~brobst/chronicles/chap2.htm

45 http://www.eyewitnesstohistory.com/passage.htm

46 https://www.ushistory.org/us/5b.asp

47 https://www.britannica.com/biography/William-Penn-English-Quaker-leader-and-colonist

48 https://eh.net/encyclopedia/indentured-servitude-in-the-colonial-u-s/

49 http://www.emmigration.info/us-immigration-trends-1700s.htm
https://en.wikipedia.org/wiki/Indentured_servitude

50 https://images.search.yahoo.com/yhs/search;_ylt=AwrEZ6paw7Fex
H8ADA0PxQt.;_ylu=X3oDMTByMjB0aG5zBGNvbG8DYmYxBHBv
cwMxBHZ0aWQDBHNlYwNzYw--?p=german+newspapers+in+Ameri
ca&fr=yhs-elm-001&hspart=elm&hsimp=yhs-001

51 https://constitutioncenter.org/blog/april-fools-german-as-americas-official-language/

52 ht11 https://www.history.com/topics/colonial-america/plymouth#section_2

53 https://historynewsnetwork.org/article/149661

54 https://www.mentalfloss.com/article/53330/17-bizarre-natural-remedies-1700s

55 https://www.americanantiquarian.org/proceedings/44807198.pdf

56 https://www.healthyhildegard.com/healing-plants/

57 www.history.com/topics/american-revolution

58 www.britannica.com/event/American-Revolution

59 https://americanexperience.si.edu/wp-content/uploads/2014/07/Loyalists-and-Patriots.pdf \

60 https://foxtrotalpha.jalopnik.com/the-revolutionary-war-by-the-numbers-1600199390

61 https://en.wikipedia.org/wiki/United_States_Army_Provost_Marshal_General

62 https://www.smithsonianmag.com/history/baron-von-steuben-180963048/

63 https://ar chive.org/stream/jstor-20083492/20083492_djvu.txt

64 https://allthingsliberty.com/2013/10/10-amazing-women-revolutionary-war/

65 https://digitalcommons.liberty.edu/cgi/viewcontent.cgi?article=1020& context=symp_grad

66 https://allthingsliberty.com/2015/05/a-quaker-struggles-with-the-war/

67 http://mennoworld.org/2016/07/04/the-world-together/to-exit-or-remain-the-july-4-1776-question/

68 https://historyofmassachusetts.org/british-army-revolutionary-war/

69 https://en.wikipedia.org/wiki/Germans_in_the_American_Revolution

70 https://graduateway.com/hessian-german-soldiers-mercenaries-revolutionary-war/

71 https://www.nps.gov/york/learn/historyculture/german-auxiliary-units-at-yorktown.htm

72 https://en.wikipedia.org/wiki/Germans_in_the_American_Revolution#Hesse-Kassel

73 https://en.wikipedia.org/wiki/Germans_in_the_American_Revolution

74 https://en.wikipedia.org/wiki/Hessian_(soldier)

75 https://www.encyclopedia.com/history/encyclopedias-almanacs-transcripts-and-maps/heister-leopold-philip-von

76 https://en.wikipedia.org/wiki/Hessian_(soldier)   https://www.mountvernon.org/library/digitalhistory/digital-encyclopedia/article/wilhelm-von-knyphausen/

77 https://www.britannica.com/place/Germany/The-1850s-years-of-political-reaction-and-economic-growth

78 https://en.wikipedia.org/wiki/German_revolutions_of_1848%E2%80%93931849

79 https://www.nber.org/chapters/c7434.pdf
https://ediblemarinandwinecountry.ediblecommunities.com/drink/german-roots-run-deep-california-wine-country

80 https://en.wikipedia.org/wiki/George_Rapp

81 https://en.wikipedia.org/wiki/Harmony_Society

82 https://www.history.com/news/americas-first-multi-millionaire-250-years-later

83 https://tshaonline.org/handbook/online/articles/fso03

84 https://jwa.org/encyclopedia/article/schurz-margarethe-meyer

85 https://www.encyclopedia.com/women/encyclopedias-almanacs-transcripts-and-maps/anneke-mathilde-franziska-1817-1884

86 https://softschools.com/facts/us_geography/brooklyn_bridge_facts/2511/

87 https://mentalitch.com/history-of-coors-beer/

88 http://www.beerhistory.com/library/holdings/millerhistory.shtml

89 https://www.anheuser-busch.com/about/heritage.html

90 https://www.pabstmansion.com/history/pabst-brewing-co

91 http://www.oldbreweries.com/breweries-by-state/wisconsin/appleton-wi-5-breweries/muench-brewery-wi-9f/

92 https://www.charleskrug.com/

93 https://www.kunde.com/About-Us/The-Kunde-Family

94 https://ediblemarinandwinecountry.ediblecommunities.com/drink/german-roots-run-deep-california-wine-country

95 https://sonomavalleywine.com/the-roots/summoning-the-dresels/#.XsK0C2hKg-E

96 https://en.wikipedia.org/wiki/History_of_American_wine

97 https://www.kunde.com/About-Us/The-Kunde-Family

98 http://www.kitchenproject.com/history/Goetta/index.htm

99 http://jewishencyclopedia.com/articles/14108-sulzberger

100 http://www.localhistories.org/americancivilwar.html

101 https://www.thoughtco.com/american-civil-war-a-short-history-2360921

102 https://www.battlefields.org/learn/articles/civil-war-casualties

103 https://www.thevintagenews.com/2018/03/01/little-drummer-boy/

104 https://blogs.loc.gov/teachers/2013/02/women-soldiers-in-the-civil-war/

105 http://sites.rootsweb.com/~kycampbe/germanscivilwar.htm

106 https://www.encyclopediavirginia.org/Sigel_Franz_1824-1902#start_entry

107 https://www.thoughtco.com/carl-schurz-2360403

108 https://en.wikipedia.org/wiki/Alexander_Schimmelfennig

109 https://www.sil.si.edu/ondisplay/caricatures/bio_nast.htm

110 https://military.wikia.org/wiki/German_Americans_in_the_Civil_War

111 http://sites.rootsweb.com/~kycampbe/germanscivilwar.htm

112 https://civilwar.wikia.org/wiki/Heros_von_Borcke

113 https://www.sil.si.edu/ondisplay/caricatures/bio_nast.htm

114 https://military.wikia.org/wiki/German_Americans_in_the_Civil_War

115 http://sites.rootsweb.com/~kycampbe/germanscivilwar.htm

116 https://civilwar.wikia.org/wiki/Heros_von_Borcke

117 https://en.wikipedia.org/wiki/History_of_Germans_in_Russia,_ Ukraine_and_the_Soviet_Union

118 https://www.history.com/topics/immigration/ellis-island

119 https://www.history.com/news/immigrants-ellis-island-short-processing-time

120 https://www.history.com/topics/world-war-i/world-war-i-history

121 https://reimaginingmigration.org/the-anti-german-sentiment-of-world-war-i/

122 https://www.history.com/news/anti-german-sentiment-wwi

123 https://www.loc.gov/teachers/classroommaterials/presentations andactivities/presentations/immigration/german8.html

124 https://academic.oup.com/restud/article-abstract/87/1/204/5472346?re directedFrom=fulltext

125 http://jbuff.com/c020713.htm juden

126 https://www.britannica.com/place/Third-Reich/The-Enabling-Act-and-the-Nazi-revolution

127 https://www.britannica.com/topic/Nurnberg-Laws

128 https://www.britannica.com/event/World-War-II

129 https://search.yahoo.com/search?fr=mcafee&type=E211US1485G0&p =treaty+marshal+plan+end+world+war+2

130 https://www.history.com/topics/germany/weimar-republic

131 https://legalinsurrection.com/2018/06/remember-the-detainment-of-ethnic-germans-in-the-u-s-during-wwi-and-wwii/

132 https://www.warhistoryonline.com/instant-articles/internment-of-germans.html

133 https://www.britannica.com/topic/German-American-Bund

134 https://www.cbsnews.com/news/wwii-us-germans-were-enemy-aliens/

135 http://www.city-data.com/forum/history/2659310-wwii-anti-german-sentiment-us-towards.html

136 https://www.smithsonianmag.com/history/stopping-nazi-plots-1930s-los-angeles-180966961/

137 https://www.thoughtco.com/german-american-bund-4684500

138 https://encyclopedia.ushmm.org/content/en/article/ immigration-to-the-united-states-1933-41

139 https://www.moving.com/tips/how-famous-american-immigrants-moved-to-us/

140 http://jbuff.com/c020713.htm

141 https://encyclopedia.ushmm.org/content/en/article/voyage-of-the-st-louis

142 https://www.vanderbilt.edu/AnS/physics/brau/H182/Term%20Papers/Eric%20Weiss.html

143 https://www.britannica.com/biography/Wernher-von-Braun.

144 https://www.nasa.gov/centers/marshall/history/vonbraun/bio.html

145 https://en.wikipedia.org/wiki/Yuenglinghttps://www.google.com/search?sxsrf=ALeKk02bLEAe_QUTUTwfp23qDBLDD09g4w%3A1590850954719&ei=inXSXs66K4O2ggfQhJSYDQ&q=yuengling+beer+history&oq=yuengling+beer+history&gs_lcp=CgZwc3ktYWIQAzICCAAyBggAEBYQHjIGCAAQFhAeMgYIABAWEB4yBggAEBYQHjoECAAQRzoHCAAQFBCHAlDMa1iEfWCx6QFoAHABeACAAAX6IAdEGkgEDNC40mAEAoAEBqgEHZ3dzLXdpeg&sclient=psy-ab&ved=0ahUKEwjOp6_Q7dvpAhUDm-AKHVACBdMQ4dUDCAw&uact=5

146 https://www.britannica.com/biography/Henry-Engelhard-Steinway

147 https://www.biography.com/fashion-designer/levi-strauss

148 https://en.wikipedia.org/wiki/Joseph_Schlitz_Brewing_Company

149 https://www.atomicheritage.org/article/scientist-refugees-and-manhattan-project

150 https://www.britannica.com/biography/Bruno-Hauptmann

151 https://www.atomicheritage.org/article/scientist-refugees-and-manhattan-project

152 https://www.passport-collector.com/us-consul-raymond-h-geist-saved-jewish-lifes-nazi-germany/

153 https://sputniknews.com/europe/201704281053100872-german-migrant-crisis/

154 https://nationalvanguard.org/2019/06/crime-statistics-in-germany/?doing_wp_cron=1591557874.1292378902435302734375

155 Leubecher, Marcel (27 April 2018). "Zuwanderer in einigen Kriminalitätsfeldern besonders auffällig". Die Welt.

156 https://www.eisenhowerlibrary.gov/eisenhowers/eisenhower-ancestry

157 https://www.offthegridnews.com/religion/worlds-christian-population/

158 https://encyclopedia.ushmm.org/content/en/article/united-states-immigration-and-refugee-law-1921-1980 http://holocausthandbooks. com/dl/12-jefttr.pdf

159 https://encyclopedia.ushmm.org/content/en/article/united-states-immigration-and-refugee-law-1921-1980

160 http://holocausthandbooks.com/dl/12-jefttr.pdf

161 https://en.wikipedia.org/wiki/Nationality_law_in_the_American_Colonies

162 https://www.lva.virginia.gov/public/guides/rn9_natural1657.pdf

163 https://en.wikipedia.org/wiki/United_States_nationality_law

164 https://www.law.cornell.edu/constitution-conan/amendment-14/section-1/citizens-of-the-united-states

165 https://en.wikipedia.org/wiki/United_States_nationality_law#Acquisition_of_citizenship

166 https://citizenshiptests.org/tests/us-citizenship-test-1800s/

167 https://www.thoughtco.com/the-history-of-naturalization-requirements-1951956

168 https://www.uscis.gov/history-and-genealogy/genealogy/historical-record-series/visa-files-july-1-1924-march-31-1944

169 https://www.pewresearch.org/fact-tank/2015/09/30/how-u-s-immigration-laws-and-rules-have-changed-through-history/

170 https://history.state.gov/milestones/1921-1936/immigration-act

171 https://en.wikipedia.org/wiki/History_of_laws_concerning_immigration_and_naturalization_in_the_United_States

172 http://evolutionofwomenscitizenship.weebly.com/colonial-era.html

173 https://blog.library.in.gov/a-brief-history-of-the-united-states-passport

174 https://www.pewforum.org/essay/the-growth-of-germanys-muslim-population/

175 https://www.statista.com/statistics/270272/percentage-of-us-population-by-ethnicities/

176 https://www.pewforum.org/2015/04/02/religious-projections-2010-2050/

Printed in the United States
By Bookmasters